The

21

Principles of a
LIE

Rodney Lee Smith

The 21

Principles of a

The Logic
of the Illogical

LIE

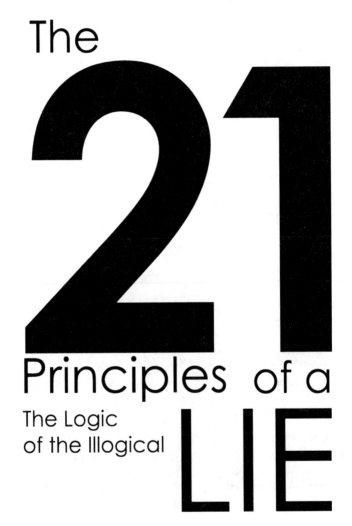

TATE PUBLISHING & Enterprises

Published by Tate Publishing & Enterprises, LLC
127 E. Trade Center Terrace | Mustang, Oklahoma 73064 USA
1.888.361.9473 | www.tatepublishing.com

Tate Publishing is committed to excellence in the publishing industry. The company reflects the philosophy established by the founders, based on Psalm 68:11,
"The Lord gave the word and great was the company of those who published it."

Book design copyright © 2010 by Tate Publishing, LLC. All rights reserved.
Cover design by Blake Brasor
Interior design by Lindsay B. Behrens

Published in the United States of America

ISBN: 978-1-61566-979-0
1. Self-Help / Personal Growth / General   2. Self-Help / General
10.02.19

"The faces and voices of liars will change but the methodical aspects of a lie will not."

Notice to Readers

Dedication

I would like to thank my loving parents Guy and Trevor Lee for their invaluable and emotional support during the penning process of this book.

In addition, I would like to thank the Reverend Clarence Watkins for his reference support in the process of finding biblical passages which helped me in my quest to find empirical support to support my beliefs according to the bible.

Table of Contents

Frame of Reference

Identifying the tactics and strategies of a liar are critical for an individual's personal security. The need to do this will become paramount if you are serious about achieving success on any level in your life. It will not matter what the local, national, or the international economy is doing; whether it is booming or stagnant. The results of not being able to identify serious liars, relationship saboteurs, head-walkers, and destroyers on a personal level will prove to be deviating for an individual who cannot identify them.

One must understand that historical facts support the concept that liars, whether they are individuals or groups, will be with us at all times and at all levels. The faces and voices may change, but the methodology will remain the same. They can or will show up in your life on many levels; whether they come as family, professional, romantic, or economic. The only way to deal with these individuals or groups is to do one of the following:

A. Purge/remove these individuals from your life. (Do not allow them into your life.)
B. Remove yourself from contact with these individuals on all levels; whether they will be family, romantic, personal, or professional who you know are engaging in acts that are not acceptable in accord to your personal morals or ethics. This is critical because the collective efforts of these individuals who knowingly participate in a lie will result in what is known as wickedness in high places.

In time, this attitude will ultimately lead to corruption by all parties on all levels of any organization. You cannot have wickedness, corruption, and the negating of leadership responsibility on the same page as moral, ethical, and legal transparency.

The concepts of wickedness and truth are diametrically opposed to one another (opposite to each other). This guiding principle applies to mankind just as basic laws of physics apply to science and numbers apply to math. Wickedness in high places will always be or have the sprit of equality as it relates to all the parties involved in the cover-up if it's ill intended. This guiding principle applies also to every aspect of leadership in government, business, or personal relationships. Wickedness in high places will always exist in the warm embrace of corruption. Corruption will only manifest its self in human environments where it is welcomed by the blessing of ownership, leadership, or managerial approval.

Once wickedness in high places occurs, the acts of corruption will soon follow and permeate every level of organizational hierarchy. The actions of these few individuals or groups will in fact be the public finger-print and signature of serious liars, head-walkers, relationship saboteurs, and destroyers.

In the work place, leadership must always take responsibility for the actions of its subordinates. When leadership in an administrative capacity knowingly negates its obligation to protect the public, its national citizens, employees, or clients, observers will have no doubt that private agendas designed to accomplish a theft at some level are in effect. The process will always embody elements of conflict of interest.

Historical facts tell us that corruption can and have in fact led to the fall of great civilizations of the world. Individuals who knowingly and willingly participate in the actions to defraud by deception using knowledge, position of power, or intentional fraud will each experience personal setbacks on many levels of their lives. (Readers: you must remember that serious liars, head-walkers, relationship saboteurs, and destroyers need not be individuals who are in your office work environment or neighborhood community alone. They can be relatives on your family tree.)

The greatest crimes that are being committed on a daily basis are not occurring on the streets of cities around the world that you see on the four, five, six, and ten o'clock television news hour.

The greatest crimes in history are being committed by individuals or groups of people who are working in offices. They can be mom-and-pop operations, working professionals, or global corporations. Some (not all) individuals who work in these environments are using office skills to pursue private agendas.

The method may take many forms including using computers, fax machines, e-mail, or telephone systems. In addition, notepads and water cooler gossip may be employed in an effort to discredit coworkers. These have always been tried and proven tactics to achieve the desired results of robbery using a lie. The robbery can even be concealed in the legal or the legislative process as a way to initiate legalized robbery of the citizens of not just one nation, but many nations. The important idea to remember is that the methodical (how) aspects of a lie will always remain the same. The act of a serious lie in time will affect the lives of people not only in their own organizations or communities, but people around the world. Later in the book I will explain what I mean by identifying people who are serious liars, relationship saboteurs, head-walkers, and destroyers.

If you are genuine about protecting yourself from negative affects of liars, you must be proactive by putting into place or having place two major things:

Support group: This group will consist of close trusted friends or associates, church leaders, professional affiliations, networking people who are not company or organizational members who you feel you can talk to about the major issues confronting you.

Stop Gates: The second will entail creating personal economic "stop gates" measures (revenue generating income investments) outside of your primary job to offset the residual effects of a serious lie and the actions of relationship saboteurs, head-walkers, or destroyers.

Time is of the essence; don't delay mastering the skill ideas expressed in this book. The ideas expressed in the following pages may prove to be more important than you think. Individuals who do not take the time to learn how to identify serious liars will repeatedly make the same mistakes in life. This will not be because they are not intelligent individuals. It will be because they have not learned how to identify serious liars. As a result, they will either invite or allow relationship saboteurs, head-walkers, or destroyers to be a part of their daily lives. There inability to identify these types of liars will often have tragic results.

"Yesterday is a canceled check; tomorrow is a promissory note; today is ready cash—use it."

Kay Lyons

Personal Acknowledgment

I would like to state at this point that the writing of this book is not my intention to give legal advice, religious guidance, or clinical support to individuals who seek or need professional help. I am not a lawyer, ordained theologian, or psychologist.

The principles described in this book are observations I have made about my personal experiences over the past twenty years. I drew upon academic and business experiences to develop these observations over time. My encounters come from land-lording for seventeen years as a real-estate investor; teaching as a classroom teacher for sixteen years; and being a business owner, M.B.A. recipient, and counselor from working in a non-profit social services agency in Gary, Indiana. In the process of reading this book, I ask that the reader view the principles expressed in the following pages as what we call in political science a perceived or assumed hypothesis.

By definition, a hypothesis is: An idea assumed to be true for the sake of argument or further study. This belief can be held by many or a select few to be true until it is rejected by empirical investigation (direct experience or observation: relying on practical experience rather than on science or theory) to be either true or false.

The Harcourt Brace School Dictionary

Upon writing this book, I ask that if you are looking for vindication or rejection of the principles expressed in the following pages, look only at the reflection you see in the mirror of yourself. Think about experiences you have had with people who were a part of your life. If these people let you down or created situations that to this day you do not understand, after reading this book, ask yourself, did they fulfill any, some, or all of the principles of a lie as listed and outlined in the following pages. If you find that the person/s in question did in fact fulfill one of the principles, then you can judge for yourself if in fact any of the other principles have merits to your personal situation and experiences in life. If you find one of the principles to be true, more than likely you will find that many more of the twenty-one principles of a lie will be applicable to events, people, and outcomes that on the surface did not seem logical in the way they were handled or turned out. However, in the end, you will be able to understand the "logic of the illogical" as it relates to the methodical approach of a lie.

My purpose for writing this book is to not only enlighten, but also raise the reader's consciousness to the point where they will be able to immediately identify the tactics and methodology of a liar.

After reading this book, you will be able to do the following:

A. Identify why the perception of privilege attracts the attention of serious liars.

B. Identify the characteristics of the Art of Conversation and Communication.

C. Identify the characteristics a lie must have.

D. Identify the five major types of lies.

E. Identify the strategic stages and strategies of the lie process.

F. Identify who the players are or were and the special interest involved.

G. Identify the lies end state goals and how it was created to negatively affect you as an individual person, group, or nation.

H. Why being placed in a hard place may not be a bad location if you identify what your rock is and approach it right.

In short, I leave the final judgment of the literary veritably of this book in the hands of individuals and the court of public opinion; for each of us will convince ourselves of whether or not the principles expressed in the following pages are legitimate and worthy of intellectual merits and discussion.

My hope is that this book will in some way assist its readers in four ways. The first will be the ability to unravel the truth behind questionable actions of individuals or groups. Secondly, understand the importance of creating the skills needed to make adjustments should the reader need time to prepare both defensive and offensive tactics to protect themselves against the effects of what I call a Living Spiritual Murder (the reality of living with the residual actions of a serious liar). Thirdly, emphasizing the need for every person to be able to identify their DNA success model. Finally, give the reader the tools they will need to help them protect their blessings.

Understanding the Process

The need to understand the methodical process of serious liars is important because it will incorporate a number of strategies using trickery, position of power, and words to create envy of others in their hearts as well as yours. Once you have read this book, you will understand that there is truly logic in the madness of a lie and that there is logic in the illogical when it comes to confronting the actions of a serious liar.

The first aspect of the author of serious lies will be that they always create the story to suit their purposes. With this in mind, the reader will see that it is vital for each individual to understand the importance of creating what business people call multiple streams of income. Because the author of a serious lie will always attempt to take some object of value in addition to both breaking and destroying relationships between the owner of the coveted possession and others.

The second aspect each of us must be willing to understand is that life will always be full of challenges. Many, if not most, of these challenges you will not be able to prevent. These challenges will ultimately make you a stronger person and give you the ability to endure new challenges you will face in the future.

The third aspect of understanding the principles of a lie is to make aware to the reader the need to not fulfill any of the first twenty of the twenty-one principles explained in this book.

Doing so will always bring about problems in your personal life. Additional problems are something no one needs or should voluntarily want if they don't have to experience them. Most importantly, you may find that the price of association with individuals who knowingly promote a lie will be too high a price to pay personally. The knowledge of the principles of a lie is paramount in everyone's life in an attempt to help them understand the necessity of creating additional revenue streams of income. You cannot be focused on success one hundred percent of the time without being aware of the need to have a defensive strategy in place to protect yourself from economic attack from liars. The first protection (stop gates) will be prayer. Secondly, additional revenue (streams of income) you created. This will allow the individual or family to live as close as possible, the life they have come to expect, and have grown accustomed to under adverse conditions. This will give the target of a liar time to either defend or regroup themselves from the adverse residual effects of a living spiritual murder. A living spiritual murder will be the adverse conditions created in someone's life by the actions of a serious liar that did not exist before they meet them.

In an information society; where computers are commonplace and information about individuals can be marketed, sold, or disseminated around the world with the click of a mouse; the need to protect your income sources has become vital.

The most common and effective way to destroy a person in this type of work/social environment is to either enact strategies of identity theft in an attempt to become someone who you are not, or tell a lie and use false information to discredit an individual's character and abilities. The act of a lie in the present period that we live in will have its most devastating effect upon a person's finances, which in turn can affect the complete family unit as we know it. This will not only affect Americans, but people in all industrialized, technological nations of the world.

In short, you cannot depend upon your job anymore to give you security and peace of mind that your parents had, because markets change, technology changes, and individuals move around from place to place more often. With this as our background, my hope is that the reader understands the need for every individual to guard their identity on all levels in an effort to ensure economic ability to survive in the years to come.

Create Your Universe by Working Your Passion

The concept of "creating your universe by working your passion" evolved over a period of time as a result of my empirical observations of people who I viewed to be what society calls successful. My conclusion was that one of the reasons successful people are successful is because they study, learn, specialize, and master a specific skill, subject, or develop paradigm shifting (new ideas). They truly master the art of working smarter by redefining process skills and actions to achieve their goals. One of the simplest methods to achieve success is to read. Reading the newspaper daily is a great way to pick up on local trends, ideas, and create niche markets that a budding entrepreneur may be able to fulfill. Everyone has at least two gifts that they are born with and are not academically based that I feel will allow them to make substantial income if they are able to apply their skills. I call this your DNA success model, and I will discuss it later I the book. But before we begin to commence our serious study of the tactics of serious liars, we must first understand three fundamental precepts as they relate to establishing defensive tactics to protect you against the attacks of serious liars. The first I will call the perception of privilege; secondly, the Art of Conversation and Communication; thirdly, understanding the "S" factor in every one's boat of life; and finally, understanding the true meaning of being between a rock and a hard place.

It's a Two Sided Coin: Debunking Myth for Becoming Rich

The "reality" of the concept of being rich.

From time eternal, people who have had the opportunity to grow-up in capitalist societies have always strived for what many call and consider "the good life." "The good life" can be whatever you as an individual perceived it to be according to your definition of life, and as long as you are having fun with it, its legal and you are not hurting others; whether physical, psychological, or monetarily. All too often, the people in mass advertising sell the idea that "the good life" is free, easy, and without work or problems. There could be nothing further from the truth than this. For driving my point home, let us examine the concept of becoming rich in America.

Anyone who has achieved financial success will tell you that the process, unless it is inherited, is stressful, time-consuming, and requires some type of effort on the part of the individual. The other side of the coin in relations to accumulating money is the concept of being able to keep your money once you make it, so taxes and a host of service charges do not consume it. Good financial planners, attorneys, and accountants will advise their clients to make sure they have a tax plan in place to protect their assets so they do not outlive their hard-earned income now, but for future generations if it is passed on.

The "Reality" of the Concept of Success

The same holds true for the two-sided coin concept of becoming successful. Anyone who becomes successful at any level in life will attract the attention of others no matter what their skills or endeavors are. Everyone knows or feels they know that the concept of success means prosperity in whatever endeavors you are engaged in. Usually, the achievement of success will manifest itself in a number of ways; the least of which will certainly be the appearance of lifestyle changes.

Most people do not realize that the opposite side of success will have a tendency to ignite jealously in others. This feeling will be what I call a jealous-envious heart. A jealous-envious hearted person's motivation will always be self-centered in an effort to gain a position of power in an effort to be able to leverage future decisions in their favor; and secondly, to protect what they perceive to be their position of power. In addition to this process, there will always be an objective designed to tear another person or group down and increase his or her burdens.

This is the only way they can insure their position of importance concerning the justification of decisions they will make should they become the new leaders. Because the process is planned, it will always have an objective end and an end-state goal.

Because of the aforementioned psychological disposition, a jealous-hearted person or group will stoop to any level to achieve his, her, or their goals of tearing another person, group, or organization down.

This person or group will forget all issues of ethical and moral behavior in relations to how they conduct themselves. In addition, their actions need not have any rhyme or reasons for their motivation. Their overall objective is to take the personal things that they feel allow the intended victim to prosper, take them, and reap the benefits for themselves. They do not want the target-victim personally as an individual, as a general rule, they want their position, job, access to knowledge, and contacts that allowed the individual or group to be successful and enjoy what they perceived to be the "good life" as it relates to the rewards process.

Thus in hindsight, one can easily see that the jealous- hearted persons or groups have all the motivation they need to initiate the acts of what I call a serious liar. The definition of a serious liar will be explained shortly in the proceeding paragraphs. The thing to remember is that their actions will always have devastating effects upon the intended victim if they are not aware of the events accruing on around them at the same time.

The Perception
of Privilege

The perception of privilege, advantage, power, and independence are the hallmarks that successful people will manifest in their daily lives. This perception, whether it is real or imagined in the eyes of others, are the marks that make individuals or groups attractive targets to serious liars.

People who are successful will always operate on all four of the (hallmark) corners simultaneously. These success hallmarks corners are the trigger strings that will automatically ignite the feelings of hatred, jealously, envy, manipulation, persuasion, intimidation, and a need to dominate others in a serious liar.

The efforts of successful people may be classified by some as a "hustle," working hard and honestly to get a job done in an effort to achieve a selected goal by a certain time. On the other hand, a serious liar will always enact and pursue methodological (how) strategies that will be a con-game.

A con-game is designed from the beginning as a means to commit a fraud. A fraud is designed to obtain a receivership by trick, deception, or manipulation. Fraudulent activity is always committed under false pretext. A false pretext is always a reason or motive given to conceal the truth. Needless to say, the actions undertaken by serious liars will always be fraudulent, untruthful, and as a result illegal in most cases.

Serious liars will pursue any methodology to achieve their goals if they are insecure about themselves or do to know their personal DNA success model.

The desire to obtain monetary rewards need not be the driving force behind the actions of a serious liar. Serious liars will act the way they do because they have a deep inward desire to prove their self-worth to themselves as well as others. This deeply rooted insecurity complex will be the motivating factor behind their character assassination efforts of the selected target; whether they are individual or groups.

Below is the power corner diagram that I feel adequately reflects the characteristics of successful people.

Privilege   Advantage

DNA
Success Perception

Power   Independence

Skills or Ability

Privilege: Confidence, a feeling of trust; reliance; faith; not pride or arrogance.

Individuals who operate in a sprit of privilege always carry them selves with an air of confidence. They will have faith in their convictions and not use their power or position to knowingly suppress or take advantage of other in a negative way. They will not have to boost to every body about the great accomplishments they have done unless the topic or form requires the establishment or vindication of legitimacy.

Advantage: Being in your own element, not boastful. This will generally be some type of natural ability. When a person is working from their strengths, natural gifts and abilities, they will be able to do what others view as the impossible. They will make the physical or intellectual process look effortless and do it with ease. The most visible example of this can be found on the sports pages of any newspaper, television sports show or the internet were reporters write about the great accomplishment a particular individual has done whether they be male or female. On the opposite side of the page we can find examples of every one from actors to veterinarians who use office skills to accomplish their task weather they work indoors at a desk or outdoors working on a construction site and reading blueprints to survey land or lay water and drainage systems or build buildings. When a person is working or operating in their natural element (comfort zone), the chances are good that they will be successful because the process will be a natural fit for them and their personality, skills/training, and biological makeup because of who their parents were.

Power: knowing you can effect change, and make decisions based on the right thing to do and not necessarily what is popular. People who operate with a sprit of consciousness will always rebuke the actions of serious liars (authors of the madness). They will instinctively know that their actions will get many people in trouble and even question the integrity of others if the statements or actions of liars are proven to not be true. Individuals who operate in the power mode and make the right decisions, not the popular decision will in time, gain legitimacy and insulate themselves from adverse verbal or written counter attacks because there actions in most cases will prove to have been the correct decision in their attempt to move the consciousness of society forward.

On the other hand, the false doctrine of serious liars if they are in power can have the reverse affect of positive change. Serious liars who are in power will always be correct because they are the one's who are penning the story-falsehood as they want others to believe it. The process may be internal as with organizations or external with people standing in the street supporting causes that will negatively affect their own lives and beliefs. Individuals who understand the necessity to make the right decisions will be able to see the collective efforts of serious liars and identify their private agendas if they know the principles of a lie.

People who have true power will always have the skills and ability to affect positive change. Serious liars are very uncomfortable with independent /forward thinking people who operate in a sprit or moral and ethical accountability. Nobody's perfect, and at some point everyone will fall short of the grace of God, but there is a difference in being involved in events that gust happened or turn out badly because of circumstances that could not be predicted such as natural disasters of nature. Or unforeseen events that occurred that are clearly out of the ordinary and have no precedence. Individuals who use power and understand that they are accountable for their actions are different from those who are rough. There is a difference when it comes to accepting accountability of making poor decisions as they relate to events guest happening that are out of the control of the decision makers; as opposed to individuals who actively plot to intentionally put people in a hard place using knowledge, position, or power to undermine others intentionally.

If an individual does not possess the skills or ability to affect change, they will ultimately lose their credibility. Their "bark" will always be meaningless once discovered and others will know it. In addition, successful people will have a tendency to handle challenges with grace for the most part. They will not always need or be looking for recognition. Others will always know who the true power is behind the process.

Independence: Being able to think for yourself, without being intimidated by others or react to what others think or say about you.

Individuals who are successful in any endeavor in life will always operate on all four of the power corners simultaneously. They will undoubtedly attract the attention of many because many will be wondering how they were able to achieve such great success with what many may feel to be either humble beginnings or a lack of intellectual advantage. Successful people will always experience adversity in their walk in life. It comes with the territory. Anyone who is truly successful will not, most likely, be what some may call a plain vanilla personality.

A plain vanilla person will not be a bad person. They just may not go very far or achieve their true potential in life. What makes people interesting to others is their ability to overcome insurmountable odds and in the end they become the story of legends.

The history books are full of great men and women, who challenged conventional wisdom, both on and off the field; defied the odds and won where many would have surely thought that they would fail. The sports pages are full of individuals; men and women who confronted what many would believe to be insurmountable odds and somehow walked out in victory. These are the stories that inspire others, unite nations, and credit social movements, which in the end ignite the concept of a paradigm shift (Challenge and change conventional wisdom.)

They are, in fact, the true mavericks of the world. But the one quality of their lives is that they single-handedly uplift all of those around them who desire and are striving for a better life, opportunity, or peace within. They will bring new insight to old ideas, beliefs, and always blaze the new frontier, and in hindsight their journey in many cases will be a solitary pursuit.

Getting it Right

Success, for most individuals, will always be a solitary journey with many forks in the road. You may become successful with a team but, someone on the team will always be the most valuable player (MVP).

Someone will hit the winning home run ball.

Someone will make the impossible game winning catch.

Someone will score the last-second goal or basket.

Someone will finish a team rally race as first among many.

Someone will sink the impossible golf put.

Someone will deliver the closing statement that wins the contract, seals the deal, or convinces the jury in a court of law that their argument is right and present the undisputable evidence that will convince all of the validity of their position.

Someone will attach the exclamation point to a miracle finish, whether it's on or off the field, in the halls of academia, scientific, or a technological breakthrough.

People who are successful will always face challenges. If they approach the issues correctly, the challenges will enhance their personal growth development. The process and reactionary effort will allow them to claim both legitimacy and experience in an effort to prepare them for the next challenge. The fulfillment of the *Principles of a Lie,* however, will always reveal character issues (concerns). These concerns will not only reveal the worst in another person. They will be a forerunner as to alert others of their self-centered nature, capabilities, and ruthlessness.

The truly successful, at some point, will always experience personal betrayal and possible sabotage of their personal efforts from close acquaintances at the most critical point in their life journey. They should expect the unexpected when things go too smoothly. Understanding the principles of a lie will not totally remove these individuals from your life. It will, however, alert you of their tactics and allow an individual to be better prepared to meet unexpected events that are truly illogical on the surface and run counter to all theories of conventional wisdom.

The Art of Conversation and Communication

If any one is trying to or thinking of becoming successful in any aspect of your life, you must be able to identify and distinguish what the level is of the conversation you are having with any one individual. Most people become victims of serious liars because they are unable to identify the level of conversation which the speaker is functioning on.

This fundamental flaw will always lead unsuspecting individuals and groups to become totally misled. One must remember that liars obtain their legitimacy through others ignorance. The importance of this fundamental fact is paramount in relation to keeping yourself out of both physical and psychological harm's way of a serious liar.

With this as our launching pad, let us begin our investigation about the art of conversation and communication.

Open Dialogue

Open dialogue is the most basic of all levels of communication an individual human being can have. It is generally by nature considered to be a civilized one-on-one exchange. However, it can consist of multiple members in a group discussing a single topic of interest. In an open dialogue conversation, whether the discussion is verbal or written, each individual member has the right and ability to interject his or her point of view into the discussion. This ability to voice one opinion on the issue of interest legitimizes the expression "free speech." On this level, all parties for simplistic argument are in an ideal situation and are equal. No one individual is superior to the other in the group.

Open Dialogue Vindication: High

Because the ideas or topic of discussion is at the basic level of communication, the ability to asses, prove, or confirm the position of the speaker's statement is high. Generally speaking, the subject matter will not be over the heads of the listeners or parties who are present and involved in the conversation. Secondly, the need for high level research skill to confirm the truth or the speaker's statement is not needed.

Lecture

Lecture is for the most part a one way conversation. As a general rule, this type of conversation is historically given to a group who grants the speaker command of the floor voluntarily. The listener or audience may or may not be prepared for what the speaker is talking about, but the common thread of interest will unite all who patiently allow the speaker to make his or her statement. In an ideal situation, such as a classroom the listener will be required in most cases to read the lesson the night or week before the actual presentation by the speaker.

If the audience has some background about the subject of interest; the ability to assess the truthfulness of the speaker's words is a great advantage to the audience. Reality, however, must allow us to understand that this would be an ideal situation, and that in most likelihood, there will be people in the audience who are simply curious about the speaker, topic, or simply appear at any location and listen to simply pass the time away. Characteristics of a true lecture will be that the presentation will be open to all (general public) unless in a formal classroom or by invitation only environment. Secondly, everyone will not be on the same page as far as degree of background knowledge about the subject or topic of discussion.

The ideas expressed in a lecture (particularly a classroom or in a book like the Bible) can be proven to be true on the basis of historical fact, research findings, or eyewitness accounts). The story of Jesus and the woman in the street who was running from a mob because they had accused her of adultery is high because of both historical writings and eye witness accounts of events that unfolded are well documented. The ability of the common man or woman to both relate to the events and find references to support the story independently are good. Academic leaders who make reference to this passage have first hand accounts of the events of the day, the moment, and can cross reference in scripture the interrelated aspects of these accounts as they happened on many different levels across many books in the bible.

Seminar

Unlike open dialogue or lecture, seminar is a very special type of communication. In a lecture environment, as a general rule, you can have an audience who will sit quietly in their chairs and listen attentively to the speaker's remarks. The key point of reference about a seminar however is that in most cases the members of the audience will all be on the same page in relation to a certain basic level of academic or individual knowledge about the topic being discussed. A seminar will not be the place for a novice. Unless the attendee is extremely knowledgeable by being self-read, the topic of disputes of interest to one another within their success will be so complex that the average person who walks into the meeting off the street will find that the speaker is talking about something that is completely over his or her head. They will not understand the integral fine points of his discussion as it relates to the topic that the speaker is addressing.

Examples that can be easily understood would be if an average individual walked into a convention that was being held by the American Medical Association, American Bar Association … etc.

The likelihood that the average individual would understand the vocabulary jargon of the profession as it relates to how members of the profession communicate points of interest to one another within their select profession may overwhelm any individual who did not have what is called prerequisite foundation classes in order for them to follow along with what the speaker is saying.

Individuals who attend seminars will usually have some type of advanced study or research knowledge. This basic understanding will give the listener the foundation needed to allow them to assess the accuracy of the speaker's statements. This is a major distinction that separates the novice from the learned specialist.

Slick Campaign

This is the most sophisticated level of conversation the average person will ever encounter. Unlike any of the pervious conversation definitions, a Slick Campaign will always be directed by someone and the listener as a general rule cannot assess in most cases the truthfulness of the speaker's statements. Depending on the topic and how it's presented; Slick Campaigns may even fool skilled professionals if the tactical methodologies are sophisticated enough. True unethical Slick Campaigns are by their very nature designed to always wow the individual listeners, viewers, or audience and intentionally mislead everyone.

The speaker will always have insider knowledge about the subject matter that the average person does not have. The presentations will be cleaver, ingenious and appear to be plausible to the non-assuming listeners. The presentation will always be smooth, and demonstrate a very high level of sophistication in the way it was created, its presentation techniques, and the orator's command of both the words they use and the facts they present in a certain chronological order which will always be on a high level of psychological understanding.

Let it be known, Slick Campaigns do not have to be fancy print, internet, radio, or television creations. They do not have to be high-gloss book covers, advertising ads in magazines, or high-tech billboards along the roadside that you may pass on your journey of life. Slick Campaigns in their basic and most effective methods will be on a conversational one-on-one level. The methodical nature of the effort can be as unassuming as the soft voices of two people talking to one another or the use of the microphone to address the masses; whether it's a school pep-really or an international policy proposal being presented at the United Nation in New York City.

However, the listener or audience will always be at a disadvantage if they do not have a method to simply vindicate whether or not what the speaker is saying is true or a total falsehood. Thus vindication by outsiders will for all intents and purposes, always be low. This inability to assess the legitimately of the statements can lead many astray. The act can accrue on an individual level among best friends, lovers, or even coworkers. And go all the way to the point of misleading the masses by global corporations or even appointed or elected governmental officials who will be in acting what many may call policy implementation.

The most elitist of those who can command the world stage are politicians, entertainers, writers, and Olympic or professional athletes. Because of their close working relationship with the media, they can and will have instant command of the world stage because they either become or are viewed as being iconic figures in and of themselves. The vocal expression of their opinions can smooth or rattle the emotional feather of many and thus fuel or extinguish popular beliefs that are either important to themselves or ignite issues which are viewed by society as being controversial according to general norms of society of the day. Because these individuals are easily recognized, they can create or produce popular forms of artistic expression or raise the bar in the human life experience in the field of their specialization.

Word of Fairness

Not all Slick Campaigns are frauds. They may well be simply well written (topics) with the intent to capture the potential reader's interest and are simply packaged within an effort to be visually pleasing to the eye and ear or the listener. However, Slick Campaigns do not always have to be a physical product. A Slick campaign becomes fraudulent when the intent of the creator or author at some point intentionally designed the effort to mislead the listener, reader, or viewer. The idea and content will consequently be a well organized verbal strategy to intentionally mislead the listener audience into relinquishing some form of ownership they may presently control. The ability of the listener to be able to assess the psychological method lies of this type of speaker becomes immeasurable in any attempt to assess the speaker's statements. Needless to say, the skills needed to assess others' level of conversation and methodology of communication are an obvious necessarily if you are going to protect yourself vested interest as an individual and protect themselves from harmful actions of others.

Verbal Vindication of Slick Campaigns: Low or Cannot Be Confirmed

The verbal or written effort of a Slick Campaign will always stress the greatness of infinite possibilities or lack of possibilities others will face if they don't act in a timely manner according to someone's elapsed timeline. In an attempt to solidify their base of power, elevate their self-proclaimed idea of importance, they will use any number of strategies to deflect inquiring minds about the legality of their statements. Their ideas will always be the latest-greatest. They will attempt to use guilt as a way to sway individuals into believing that if they don't act now; they will lose the chance of a lifetime. They will always play the "what's best for the family," "it's in your best interest," and "Where do you see yourself five or ten years from today" angle.

Physical Product Vindication Level of Slick Campaigns Low

In some cases, the litmus test of a product Slick Campaign is that the speaker at the end of the presentation will or may ask for a large sum of money from the audience if it's a physical product. In this case, the ability of the average listener to vindicate the authenticity of he author's position will be low in that they will not be able to immediately and independently verify the virility of the speaker's words or claims of the product.

The product is designed to wow the audience first and foremost. Individuals who work in the profession that the speakers is addressing have a much better chance of accessing the accuracy of the speakers statement and ability of the product to perform as the speaker insists it will. Once again, these individuals will be working with advanced knowledge and insider connections as a general rule.

Assessing the Process

Knowing the level of conversation will allow the individual to determine if the speaker is being truthful with them; if the listener finds himself or herself in a discussion with a speaker who is talking about something that is way over their heads. If this happens, it is best to tell the speaker "I'll think about it," and quickly remove yourself from their presence. Ideally, the best approach is to never talk to them again if you don't feel comfortable or that you are being pressured into something you don't understand or instinctively don't like. If you have to engage them again, do not allow them to talk you into something until you have had ample time to do what we call in real-estate due diligence (research the facts for yourself about the subject or topic of interest). Only then can you make a wise and intelligent decision about the level of conversation or the type of lie that is about to be instantiated against you should this be your case.

Understanding the "S" Factor in Everyone's Life.

Throughout this book I will repeatedly refer to serious liars as the Authors of the Madness. The Authors of the Madness are the individuals who intentionally "S_ _ _" in everyone else's boat of life.

The point I wish to make is that these individuals represent what I call the two-per-center group. They are the ones who knowingly put people in a hard place.

They will use there position, knowledge, and connections to create circumstances that normally would not occur in another person's life. These individuals who I referred to as the Authors of the Madness are all over the place. It must be remembered that ultimately, Authors of the Madness will within time become (what I call Rot-a-derp) destroyers. The term rot-a-derp may sound new but it is actually the word predator spelled back words. I believe the term clearly fits the methodical actions of destroyers who operate at the level of doing what ever it takes to achieve their end state goal.

They will have private agendas and are always looking out for themselves in an attempt to gain some type of receivership for personal gratification whether it's in the name of the individual or organization.

At some point an individual will either ask or wonder about the following question as it relates to identifying the Authors of the Madness.

How does one know if they are in fact fulfilling the principles of a lie?

If you are knowingly and actually engaged in the plotting of the downfall of another person and have either a direct or indirect input into the circumstances of their difficulty that otherwise would not exist without you being a part of the process. In addition, receivership by twisting the law or negating legal, moral, and ethical responsibility at some level that allowed for the obtaining of selected targets ownership. These are the hallmarks, litmus tests, and marks of vindication that identify serious liars as the Authors of the Madness and ultimately destroyers. The statements by serious liars who are the Authors of the Madness will always be true from their perspective, because they are the writers who are penning the sentences, paragraphs, and chapters in the books and ideology of the finished text in an effort to convince others of their position as it relates to a particular situation. The problem, however, will be that their actions will always be riddled with deception in an attempt to mislead others as to the true nature of any issue. Authors of the Madness will always create a physical as well as psychological climate of adversity among others who are around them. In this context, the use of conventional wisdom will not be applicable or practical because everything in the immediate environment concerning the topic at hand will both appear and in fact be illogical. At this time, I want to clarify several key points that I feel are paramount in our attempt to understand the seriousness of the actions of Authors of the Madness. First and foremost, we must remember that the Authors of the Madness are not an exclusive club, fraternity, sorority, civic, or social organization. Their members can come from highly respected families who many would believe to be pillar's of the community. They can also come from families who have a notorious historical background. They can wear the badge of law enforcement, be your child's teacher, or school administrator. They can be your favorite political, church, community, civic, or business leader. They can even be your husband or wife who lives under the same roof with you twenty-four hours of the day. The point to remember is that the Authors of the Madness are all over the place. Their faces and professions may change, but their methodological strategy will never change. It must be remembered that ultimately, Authors of the Madness will become true destroyers who have private agendas. They will always be looking out for themselves in an attempt to gain some type of receivership for personal gratification whether it's in the name of an individual or organization.

Once serious liars/Authors of the Madness realize that they have been discovered for who they really are, they will have a tendency to do one of several things to save face for themselves.

A. They will suddenly or unexpectedly disappear without reason or warning from people who question their actions or intentions.

B. They will have a tendency to blame others for their problems, events, or misdeeds that happen under their direct control if they are trying to get some type of receivership.

C. They will attempt to bluff their way out of the predicaments they created by citing time, law, or unfortunate natural events as the cause for their decision.

The problem, however, will be that they will always be one hundred percent guilty of creating the adversity in other peoples lives because of their actions using persuasion, manipulation, private agendas, greed, neglecting responsibility for others, and a desire for power will be apparent. This mixture of intoxicating psychological ingredients will always have a preplanned methodology that will be designed from its inception to achieve a selected end state goal whether its spoken or written it will be understood by all the members of the undermining parties involved or a select few who unknowingly became participations in the deception.

A Rock and a Hard Place

At some point, every one will experience adversity in life. When this happens you must understand that you may not be able to rely on conventional wisdom as defined by man to get yourself or your family through whatever challenge you may face, because the external environment will truly be illogical. You will, in most cases, not be able to distinguish friend from foe and you may even find yourself making popular decisions versus the right decisions. When this happens to you, and you find that you are the focus point of questionable allegations from serious liars; you must understand that morality, ethics, rules of behavior as they relate to how people are suppose to act toward one another as outlined in the latter five commandments of the Bible will be thrown out the window, along with the baby's dirty bath water and soiled diapers.

The actions of serious liars will always be and have a negative effect on the lives of those they target and the final result of their actions will always be devastating.

They will intentionally put people in a "hard place" on purpose and ultimately become the true "Jerks in Heels."

A Hard Place Defined

The existence of a "hard place" can best be described as follows. The creation of a situation, events, or outcomes that did not exist or had very little chance of existing in another person's life before you or any one else became a part of their lives and produced negative outcomes under which they now have to live. Individuals who knowingly engage in activities which either directly or indirectly put others in "hard places" are not only serious liars; they are in fact Authors of the Madness and ultimately destroyers. They know what they are doing and it's a true conscious effort. Their actions are not haphazard, coincidental, random accuracies, or acts of nature.

Authors of the Madness will intentionally put people in both a state of physiological and psychological freefall. At some point, the target individuals or group of people are going to hit the surface of mother earth either physically, psychologically, financially, or maybe all three.

Landing on Sand

When you hit mother earth, you will land on one of five possible surfaces. The list is not in any particular order, but you will irrevocably land on one of them. For the sake of this argument, let us say that the first surface you land on will be sand. If you land on sand, conventional wisdom would lead us to believe that our landing will be soft. However, depending on the height of the location from which you started, this may or may not be true. The fact is that if you land on sand, it's unstable and can shift. Architects and builders (who act in an ethical manner) will not build on sand unless they are able to securely anchor the building several feet below the surface on some type of bedrock or deep immersion. If they try to anchor the building to the top layers of the surface and only go a few feet down in to the ground, they know that the building will not be stable; it will shift and the building will be unstable and the dewing thus unsafe. Secondly, sand can be blown away. You only have to look at the sand dunes of most costal locations around the world or the sand dunes of the Sierra Desert in North Africa to see evidence of this fact. In addition to the two previous mentioned facts, sand can be washed away by the currents of water whether they or small lakes or the sea shores next to the ocean. Many cities who have water shore lines now find themselves facing shore erosion problems as water levels rise as a result of global warming.

Landing on Dirt

Many people may believe that landing on dirt can be a safer alternative if sand poses the problems that it does. The problem with this idea is that dirt is similar to sand in one regard and different in another. If you have high enough wind, dirt, like sand, can be blown away. The trees and crops that are planted in the ground will eventually die because there is nothing to anchor the plants to the ground, the roots system will not be able to hold water for the plants to the get liquid. The dust bowl storms of Oklahoma and Texas are prime examples of this natural phenomenal occurence and the eventual devastation of both plants and livestock in the region. The second problem with dirt is that if you get too much water on the ground, dirt will become mud. If you put your foot in it, you will get stuck and may or may not be able to get out. Worse-case-scenario is that you will actually sink down in it.

Landing on Water

If you fall and land on water, your rate of survival may not be any more assured than either sand or dirt. Depending on the height from which you started falling and the area of the country that the water is in, hitting water will or may actually cut and tear flesh just like a liquid power chain saw. Needless to say, water, just like sand, is truly not stable. In fact, of all the elements mentioned so far, water is the most unstable of them all. In the Bible it is recorded that two men actually walked on water. But, one must remember that only one of those men could do it on his own without the others' encouragement and one of them did in fact eventually fall into the water.

Landing on a Rock

The last aspect of mother earth that a person can land on is a rock. Conventional wisdom tells us that if you land on a rock, it will be painful and hurt a lot. In the physical context of what we (man) know as a human being, most people would agree that this principle would usually be very true. However, individuals who understand that if the Authors of the Madness create "hard places" in other peoples lives the rock may in fact be the best place you can land.

Landing on the rock does not mean that you will automatically land on your stomach or your back and be physically broken into thousands of tiny pieces. You will be broken in the ways of the world that you once knew or people that you once trusted. But the truth is that you may actually land on your feet. When you are faced with the concept of a "rock and a hard place" you may be in the best place you can be in. Does this mean that you will not suffer; no. Does this mean that you will not have problems; no. You must remember that the "hard place" will always be in front of you. The rock will always be behind you.

For some people the rock may stand for perseverance, commitment, determination, or even involvement to complete a task or right a wrong. Others will view the rock quite differently—they will reach back and embrace the rock behind them and view it as a protectorate. If your turn around and embrace the rock as a protectorate, you will also acknowledge it as simply the Word of God, the Laws of Moses, and the principles, pledges, promises, and resources of the Bible itself. If you embrace the rock as the pledges of God, you can rest assured that no force on earth will be able to stand against the power of the most high. The concept of the Rock is a very interesting statement in and of itself. Geologists have traced rock samples found in many parts of the world to millions of years; one such place is present day Death Valley, Arizona. If you believe that God created the earth, then the present day rocks that you can walk on in Death Valley are also a living testament to his presence today. The rocks have not changed since the day they were created and it is interesting to note that the Bible says that God's Word will not change as well. One can rest assured that the Authors of the Madness will always fulfill both part A and B of principle twenty-one. If they leave the planet and escape judgment on earth by their peers, they will not escape judgment by God for their deeds and actions on earth when they stand before him.

Words of Wisdom

In the process of penning the *Twenty-One Principles of a Lie,* I found myself repeatedly asking how the verification of the principles could be confirmed. After considerable meditation, it came to me what I had heard my parents and grandparents occasionally reiterate to me the fact that there are certain things a friend or honest person will do. Likewise, there are things that a true friend or honest person will not do. With this as a paradigm foundation, I realized that the principles of a lie actually address the topic of character issues in a person in conjunction with the act of lying.

(Character: All the good as well as the bad qualities, habits, traits, etc., that go to make up the nature or worth of a particular person.) Harcourt Brace School Dictionary: Copyright 1968 by Harcourt, Brace & World, Inc. New York, Chicago, San Francisco, Atlanta, Dallas.

Serious liars will knowingly and deliberately commit a theft on some level. They will intentionally betray trusted interests and relationships. With this in mind, it became obvious that there are four major corner stones that I feel must be in place in terms of foundational support if any human relationship has a chance of either success or longevity.

Observational Relationship Chart

Without question or hesitance, one must remember that serious liars will always violate most, if not in fact each and every one, of the relationship corner stones as mentioned in the list below.

Concept #1
Truthfulness: Transparency of actions and words.
Principle Conflict # 1,6,7,8
#1. The intended target, victim, group or audience is operating in a spirit of ignorance.
#6. The lie is designed to create a stumbling block in a person's life.
#7. A lie is designed to tear a person down.
#8. A lie is designed to increase a person's burdens.

Concept #2

Openness: No hidden agendas, serious lies or psychologically closed doors in the relationship.

Principal Conflict: # 3, 13, 14

#3. Innocent as well as serious lies do not happen by chance. They all have an author and they always have an ultimate objective.

#13. The authors or perpetuators of a serious lie never see either the moral or ethical conflict of their actions by claiming it was done and justified for the good of the group, institutions, society, or even the nation.

#14. The actions of a liar are easy to spot; Their actions never match their words. Their words never match their actions.

Concept #3

Reason: Being fair with others.

Principle Conflict: # 12, 13, 16

#12. All lies have some order of betrayal (personal) by close parties involved, who are associated with them in exchange for perceived legitimacy of value of the accusations.

#13. The author or perpetuators of a serious lie never see either the moral or the ethical conflict of their actions. They will always defend their actions by claiming it was done and justified for the good of the group, institutions, society, or even the nation.

#16. Because a lie is a deception, designed to gain the attainment of an object of desire by the author of a serious lie, they will attempt to use one or all three of the following methods to obtain ownership. Trickery, persuasion, or cohesion.

You cannot ever please a serious liar, relationship saboteur, or destroyer.

Concept #4

Commitment: Support others who support you (keep it legal), giving fully of one's self, being obligated, getting involved, assuming responsibility, and being accountable.

Principle Conflict: #12, 17.

#12 All lies have some order of betrayal (personal) by close parties involved, who are associated with them in exchange for perceived legitimacy of value of the accusation.

#17. A level two lie must always become public in order for it to gain momentum and accrue some sort of legitimacy.

Commitment evaders always want a quick exit plan in any relationship, so that they will not be accountable for anything or to anyone.

With this as our relationship criteria, it is easy to understand that serious liars will, individually or in groups, fulfill all the principles of a lie because their intent is to commit fraud from the very beginning because they are the Authors of the Madness. (Fraud: The deceiving of another for one's own gain; dishonest deception. A thing that deceives or is not genuine; trick or deception. (3) U.S. informal: A person who is not what he represents himself as being).

Needless to say, the actions of serious liars, relationship saboteurs, head-walkers, and destroyers will always reveal in time the issues of character flaws and conflict of interest. Likewise, they will always act in a spirit of dishonesty.

According to the dictionary honesty is defined as:

(Acting honorably and justly; not lying, stealing, cheating: (2) Truthful, genuine, or fair. Harcourt Brace School Dictionary: Copyright 1968 by Harcourt, Brace & World, Inc New York, Chicago, San Francisco, Atlanta, Dallas.

Serious liars will always pursue strategies that are intentionally designed to slander another (Slander: a false, spoken statement or report that harms another's reputation or prevents him from carrying on his work. The act of making such a statement publicly to make or spread false and damaging statements about; defame) individuals or selected groups in an effort to commit a theft or cover an act of wrong doing.

In the eyes of serious liars, the methodical process will justify what ever cost is incurred in the process of obtaining receivership of their perceived object of value or removing the threat of exposure of past act of wrong doing.

Serious liars will act in a brave manner because they feel that their position of power or access to knowledge will enable them to get away with acting unfairly.

Once an individual understands this fundamental fact, they will be able to see that the thread that binds the entire above relationship concepts, one through four, is time. Serious liars must always operate in an environment where others are ignorant of the facts, issues, or consequences of their actions. Ignorance basically means that you don't know not knowing something. It does not mean that you are dumb or unintelligent. Some individuals also believe that serious liars have an advantage because they gain the intended target's trust. Although trust I believe does play a part, the process of initiating the acts that eventually take something of value from another person. The concept of trust if you look it up in the dictionary conveys that the individual in my opinion is acting on some idea of perceived knowledge. This measurement may be based on personal referrals from friends or acquaintances about an individual's abilities or character.

Research what the individual has done of his or her own in accord to facts that they have come to believe as true as they relate to the world's definition of conventional wisdom. When accessing the legitimacy of someone's work, statements or position always inquire about how they developed their beliefs, strategy or methodology of interpretation of facts, events or outcomes that support their claim or position. It must be understood that trust and ignorance are two completely different words with different meanings. Serious liars do not want to, as a general rule, gain your trust one hundred percent. To do so would mean that they would have to reveal more of themselves than they would be comfortable with. This act of revealing will in time truly expose a serious liar for who he or she is, and in most cases reveal their end state goal. A serious liar must operate in a mode of secrecy and time compression. Time is not a friend to a serious liar; it's an enemy.

Serious liars operate on two fronts for the most part. The first one is ignorance and the second can be greed on the part of the victim if they are expecting some type of receivership for their actions.

The compression of time is the only factor that serious liars have to work with in their attempt achieve their goals. Because they want to mislead as many people as they can in the shortest amount of time without being exposed. They will violate all of the relationship concepts listed earlier in the observational relationship chart. If you don't have these five concepts present in any relationship, you cannot move the yardstick of life forward as it relates to human interaction with this person. This basic fundamental fact will affect relationships on all levels, whether they are personal, romantic, professional, or business.

What a Liar Really Wants

People who fall victim to a liar seldom realize what the true goal of a liar is. To understand this concept I will use both military and civilian examples to address and give understanding to the operational tactics of a liar. First let us examine how military operations work in battle. When a conquering nation invades another country, they not only want to physically take control of the country, they also want to capture the leadership of the country. This is not only a strategic necessity, but a legalizing act which the victor nation can use not only to show the conquered citizens who is in charge, but insure that the leadership does not escape into exile in a foreign country and lead revolts from abroad by the regime's supporters who are still living in the country. A liar will use a different approach; they do not want the individuals in question, their kids, or even their personal positions of success. They want the power position, which they feel allowed the target individuals to live the lifestyle or enjoy their position of decision making to effect change.

Secondly, they want the revenue producing assets of the individual. If they have this; the cars, boats, houses, etc. will come naturally later. If they have the revenue producing assets that they feel are the success contributors to the individual's success, they in fact have in their opinion, killed the targeted person of their hatred. To put this in street terms, "they want your stuff" as it relates to policy formulation and execution powers.

A liar will develop and follow what I call the "Three P's" in relation to ranking objects of desire. The first "P" deals with the concept of Power and the decision-making authority that goes with it. People who are decision-makers have unquestionably great latitude in directing the path of their business, organization, or concerns of a selected group who have common interest. Because this power ability gives the leader not only the right, but the ability to create both moral and ethical standards for its followers, employees, investors, and shape public opinion; the impact of their decisions can be paramount. Serious liars will always crave positions where the elements of power can be greatest about its ability to affect the greatest number of people.

The second "P" I labeled as the concept or ability to create their universe to a limited extent. A person who has peace of mind does not worry about external events as most people do in the world. Part of the big reason for this is that they many times will control the means of production, communication, and finance on an earthly level and have a genuine spiritual base to draw from.

These individuals have a tendency to be creators by nature and are able to not only connect the dots of abstract ideas; but also develop the paradigms for which new ideas will emerge and have either a positive or a negative effect of society as a whole in the end.

The third "P" I call the "P-F" (Power/Financial) concept.

This idea centers on the ability of creative people to be able to create revenue-generating models, which enhance their personal lives and the lives of those around them.

The combination of these "P's" create a powerfully alluring target for those who feel left out of the creative/ownership process or cannot create their own universe to bring about success in their personal lives.

Individuals or groups who fall into this category will thus be prime candidates for clandestine operations in an attempt to manipulate and defraud others of their rightly earned success and opportunities. The challenge then becomes for each individual to develop observation skills to alert him or her when confronted with events, statements, or hearsay which they feel to be questionable.

When you understand the six types of lies, you will be able to identify both the tree and fruit of a liar. The author, tree, and fruit of a lie will always be the same in terms of originality.

Historical Conceptional Framework of a Serious Lie

A Liar must always know or assume with some degree of confidence that his/her intended target, group, or audience is ignorant to some degree about the facts, issues, their rights, or the relevance of the situation at the present or historical time in order to successfully pull off a lie. Secondly, the act of a lie does not have anything to do with formal education. An individual can be a rocket scientist or brilliant brain surgeon and be misled by a six-year-old child when it comes to playing a game of chess, if the adult has never played the game before.

To begin the process of identifying the concep-tional framework of a lie, I had to first define what type of lies people tell. I concluded that there are five basic types of lies that most people tell or know about. The first I call an Innocent Lie.

The second: A Big Lie. The third: A Serious Lie. The fourth: Lie of Avoidance/Betrayal. The fifth: Time Bandits.

Innocent Lie: An innocent lie is a lie that the author of a lie tells someone to protect his or her feelings. Guiding principles of an innocent lie are as follows: The author of an Innocent Lie cannot benefit from the lie. The author does not mean ill will toward the person in question, and finally, the author does not have a hidden agenda. The author of this type of lie must always use discretion when addressing the proper time to use it.

Examples would be that an adult would not tell a young child certain things if they did not feel they could handle the subject matter. Although this type of lie involves a cover-up; no ill-will is intended and the author of the lie cannot benefit from the concealment.

There is a difference between protecting someone under the disguise of an Innocent Lie by employing the position that they are helping a friend by withholding information so that personal, emotional, or physical injury will not occur and becoming an accessory or co-conspirator to the cover-up of a crime, which is illegal.

Big Lies can be classified as almost humorous in nature. These are lies that people tell each other in a joking manner. These parties know or assume to know that there is no way that the issue or event they are talking about will ever happen. This type of lie will not as a given rule travel outside the inner-circle of friends who are joking about the topic or issue at hand. In addition, this type of lie does not have an end-stated goal and can not harm, nor is it intended to harm, anyone emotionally, financially, physically, or psychologically. The best place to find Big Lies enacted is to visit a comedy club.

Serious Lies: A serious lie on the other hand will be the exact opposite of an innocent lie and it is not a joke. This type of lie will always be selfish, mean-spirited, and have an end-state goal or object. This type of lie always involves a theft of some type on some level and will always evolve aspects of a cover-up for personal power, political, or business advantages.

Because the author of a serious lie intends to steal an object of value; the author of a serious lie will attempt to do it by one or a combination of three things:

A. Steal a selected object of desire.
B. Assume ownership of the object of desire.
C. Break and destroy relationships between parties of interest.

Because serious lies are mean-spirited and will incorporate the acts of stealing, breaking, and destroying relationships; the actions of individuals who knowingly go along with and promote this effort will always have a master plan to create hardship on the targeted group or audience. A serious lie as a result will always have the characteristics of a living "last will and testament."

By this I mean that the lie (itself) will direct the actions of the liar. Their will be a benefactor. However, the person in question (granter/target) will be very much alive. One must remember that serious lies do not happen by chance; as a result, likewise, the goal of a serious lie need not always be monetary. The theft can be centered on stealing a person's time, trust, peace of mind, opportunities, intellectual ideas, their physical freedom, or even life itself.

In addition, one must remember that because the motivation of a serious liar is selfish, their actions will always benefit only one person or the special wants and needs of a select group of people. Needless to say, the result of their actions will undoubtedly never be beneficial to either the public or the advancement of humanity on a consciousness level on any issue.

Because of the selectivity of either the author of serious lies or the special interest group associated with the act; one can easily conclude how the actions of either a single individual or select group can lead to the creation of private agendas which in turn will develop into the concept of wickedness in high places. This wickedness in high places will subsequently lead to corruption among the members within civic organizations, the family unit, public schools, corporations, law enforcement, and elected government officials.

Corruption at any of these levels will have a negative impact upon the citizenry of any location by creating unfair civil or governmental policy. To begin, I would first like to address the five categories that lies manifest themselves in. The fundamental focus of this book is not about innocent or big lies, words a liar uses, or how to read a person's body language. This book is about the methodology (how components) of what I call tactics of master/serious liars, and how to identify their strategies so individuals can protect themselves against unwanted personal, physical, psychological, or financial harm. With this in mind, one can see that the necessity to protect your blessings is paramount just for survival. After much consideration, I developed the following foundation about what I believe a true lie is in our present time.

Methodical Aspects of a Serious Lie

A Serious Lie: Is a lie which is developed by a liar from its conception, as a planned act to use knowledge and falsehood to take advantage of the ignorance of its intended victim or group. In addition, their actions are to knowingly defraud others of ownership rights, position or possessions. In addition, the desire to not only break, but destroy relationships between parties of interest in an attempt to gain a position of power for themselves.

In the dictionary, many words are used to try to convey the ideas of a lie. However, if one breaks down the words used to define a lie in accordance with the dictionary, anyone can quickly see that falsehood leads to deception, which ultimately leads to hidden agendas.

These hidden agendas will always have at their roots a desire to obtain ownership of something owned by another person. In addition, desires to not only break, but also destroy the relationships between two or more people or interest groups become paramount. The act of the destruction as it relates to this point in time will be to intentionally and permanently severe any possibly of renewing the pervious relationship. This is important because it is the only way to insure for the liar security of their future actions and survival.

Traditional Definitions of a Lie

Explanation 1. A lie is an intentionally false statement: used with reference to a situation involving deception or founded on a mistaken impression.

Concise Oxford American Dictionary:
Oxford University Press

Explanation 2. A lie is an untrue statement made with intent to deceive.

Merriam Webster Desk Dictionary

Explanation 3:
   A. A false statement purposely put forward as truth: Falsehood.
   B. Something meant to deceive or give a wrong impression.
   C. To present false image or impression.

D. To cause to be in a particular condition or affect in a specific way by telling lies: an untrue declaration.

Webster's II New College Dictionary

Explanation 4. A false statement made with deliberate intent to deceive.

Random House Webster's Dictionary
Fourth Edition

Explanation 5. To make a statement that one knows is false. To bring, put, accomplish etc. by lying. A false statement made with intent to deceive.

The Harcourt Brace School Dictionary 1968
Harcourt, Brace & World, Inc.

In the process of developing the conceptional framework for this book, I realized that traditional historical definitions of what constituted a lie did not fit the needs I had to use to appropriately convey what I felt was the true principles of a lie in twenty-first century context.

To begin with, my research and experience revealed that the traditional approach to defining a lie only covered one aspect of what was a much broader conceptional framework. To begin, one must first acknowledge that a lie is a combination of a number of interrelated shortfalls that the liar sees in themselves. This group of characters consists of jealousy, envy, resentment, and greed to name only a few. If we were to break down the following words, we would see that each has the following meaning.

A. Jealousy: Begrudging someone what he has; envious.

B. Envy: Appealing; of discontent or jealousy aroused by the good fortune or superior ability of another. A desire to have in equal amount or degree of the possessions or good qualities of another.

C. Resentment: Anger and ill-will based on real or imagined wrong or injury.

D. Greed: A selfish and grasping desire possessions, especially money.

(The Harcourt Brace School Dictionary, copyright 1968 by Harcourt, Brace & World, Inc.)

Because each of us has to some degree all of the characteristics previously mentioned and many others that are not mentioned; the stage is set for anyone to become a serious liar whether by choice or accident. The object of igniting the lie is today the same as it has been historically, "the tongue." By definition, a lie is defined as a falsehood. This falsehood uses deceit as a way to reflect attention away from the person in question. Although this is historically true, I have con-

cluded that a lie in fact is made up of five distinct parts
or levels.

The first level I will call and refer to in the
remainder of this book as a serious lie.

"The cruelest lies are often told in silence."
Robert Louis Stevenson

Level One of a Serious Lie

This lie embodies the basic historical understanding of what many people know or perceive to be the essence of a lie. This premise states that a lie is an attempt to distance or remove one's self from association with individuals, groups, time, or events of a particular nature. Classic examples of this are found in both historical and present day newspaper and magazine articles. The most common example is the story where a man or woman has been accused of committing a crime and the person in question states, "I was not at the scene of the crime, I have an alibi," or "I did not know the victim," or "I did not commit the crime."

A second aspect of a level one lie centers on promoting one's self. The fundamental attribute of this aspect of a level one lie is that it will be a cover-up and remain a secret with the author who created it. The author of a level one lie intends to promote him or herself. They will have a personal relationship with the lie and thus will not want to invite, review, or investigate into its origin, content, or validity.

Although there are exceptions to every rule, the level one type of lie is usually used to promote the authors themselves and will not as a rule take from or affect others in a negative way. Exceptions to this rule, however, will be if the author of a level one lie uses their position to draw attention to their works by creating turmoil around them. In addition, they will also create turmoil in the lives of others in an effort to impress superiors or family members in regards to their ability to solve problems that they themselves created in the first place. These individuals are always master/ serious liars who are the true Authors of the Madness. Authors of the Madness will always have an uncanny way of guaranteeing the end-state goal because they are the one who penned the script or events of the turmoil.

On the other hand, if others are involved, the circle of interest in promoting the level one lie will all have self-vested interest in the lie in order to reap personal benefits for the members in the group. This circle of friends will in most cases not exceed two or three people at the maximum, because exposure may or could lead to the legal action and possible imprisonment of the authors or collaborators if ever revealed. Common examples of level one liars would be the following:

people who falsify their resumés, computer hackers, people who are involved in hostile business takeovers, administrators, superiors, and managers who use their positions to ruin workers careers are just as guilty when authorship of the madness is confirmed. They will attempt to achieve this by making a subordinate look ineffective as a way to prove their self-worth.

A level one lie will always be covert (secret) in nature from its conception, execution, and final conclusion, which will be the attainment of what is called in graduate business schools pre-determined end-stated goals of a strategic plan. I use this loosely from a terminology standpoint; it does not mean all end-stated goals are lies.

Level Two of
a Serious Lie

Level two serious lie will be the exact opposite: where the level one lie will be covert (secret); the level two lie will be overt (in the open). The reason for this is that in order for the level two lie to achieve legitimacy and obtain its end-state goals it must gain a following in its efforts to rally supporters; whether they be willing, unwilling, or unknowing participants in the execution of the lie. The only similarity that level one and two lies have in common is that in the initial stage (stage one see page 156), the lie's authors will try every effort to remain anonymous. After this point, a level two lie must have public support in order to gain any semblance of legitimacy. In both cases, it must be remembered that a lie, whether it is a level one or level two in nature, must have an author who created the lie in the first place to smear a person's or specific interest groups' reputation. Lies do not just happen by themselves out of thin air. A second aspect of both level one and level two lies are that they must and will in all cases have an end-stated goal. This end-stated goal is the essential purpose of the lie in the first place. A lie is thus created in the first place, to insure by as close of a guarantee as possible the desired outcome of a selected course of action in an effort to achieve a select goal. In both cases, whether the serious lie is a level one or level two in concept, a cover-up-theft will accrue. The basic premise of any lie centers around three fundamental objectives.

Objective A: To take ownership away from the original owner of an object of desire using acts of trickery.

Initially this will be done using subtle tactics of persuasion. The objective is to get the owner to voluntary relinquish his/her or their (group) interest, authority, or ownership in the object of interest by appealing to the weak points of the individual or group. The use of subtle cohesion to achieve the end-state goal at this level may evolve some type of perception on the part of the individual or group that they will be receiving a personal gain. This strategy may take many forms. Examples may manifest themselves as job benefits, privileged information, and tangible objects such as money or some combination of the aforementioned list. It must be remembered that Eve took the fruit because she was anticipating obtaining some type of receivership as a result of her actions.

Objective B: *Become the new owner; tactics at this level may be more overt.* This level can or will lead to the use of many innovative tactics by a liar. The uses of aggressive strategies such as blackmail are not out of the moral or ethical boundaries in an attempt to persuade others to go along with the falsehood. The obtainment of the goal will justify, in their eyes, any efforts needed to gain the object of desire.

Objective C: To break and destroy the converted ownership relationship bond between the individuals and the object or person of specific interest.

This tactic will or can use a combination of objective A and B. If all else fails, the use of outright force or even violence may be used or enacted to achieve the desired goal of the liar if they feel that "I can get away with this." Individuals who believe this premise automatically feel that "I won't get caught." Make no mistake about it! This is both a strong and bold psychological position a liar will be in once they begin the process of perpetrating the falsehood of a serious lie.

Level Three Lie:
Avoidance [Personal]

Avoidance: This level is the hardest for most people to deal with. Avoidance was placed in this group because unlike its counterparts, level one and level two of a serious lie. The avoidance lie can be the most personally stressful because the people involved usually not only knew each other, but will in most likelihood have had a long-term, established relationships (does not have to be sexual). Because the avoidance concept centers on breaking any communication between parties of interest, it can be very hurtful to the person who feels befriended. As a landlord/property owner, I quickly learned that silence destroys relationships; this is especially true when issues of financial responsibility and repayment are in effect. When people stop communicating; the intention of one party is to avoid the other person totally. The person who initiates the silent treatment does not wish to talk to the other person because many times they feel that they (the other party) are no longer needed or of value to them, because they have gotten what they want from them. The personal avoidance act always centers around the fact that one party does not wish to communicate with the other because they do not feel they need them any longer.

Their needs have been met, and they no longer feel obligated to continue the relationship. When this occurs, a betrayal has in fact occurred and a lie was enacted because the betrayer was not open about their true feelings. Deception was used to obtain end-stated goals for their personal wants.

In short, they just went along for the ride so long as they could achieve their desired wants in the attainment process. The avoidance lie will usually take on one of three forms.

A. The first will be Personal.

B. The second will be Economic.

C. The third will be Personal or Economic Gain (Blank Check)

The economic avoidance act will usually work around the aspect of the individual breaking off communication to selected parties because they owe someone money and they simply do not have the money to pay them, their bills, rent, car payment, house payment, etc.

Level Three Lie:
Betrayal for Personal
or Economic Gain

In addition, we must also remember that the economic side of avoidance can also have polar implications as well. On one end of a pole you can have the avoidance aspects of lie present itself as a lie to avoid payment even thou financial contracts are in place and the owing party has the means and money to pay. On the other end of the pole you can have betrayal for economic gain. Betrayal for economic gain is a methodical hybrid that has the fancy name of being a "blank check". The check (information) can be sublime and trivial in nature or it can also be a slick campaign where some of the facts may be true but, only a few actually know the truth as to the verliterity of the accusation. Worse case scenario the concept of a blank check the other hand can be a total fabrication and none of the charges are true. In my opinion, blank check presenters are high class thief schemes done in a round about manner. If the check presenter approaches the target individual or group directly, with what many may call privileged information and demands payment for their silence the act will be seen by law enforcement officials as blackmail or extortion which are both illegal. Blackmail or extortion will always have economic aspects to it, and it will always be personal.

Betrayal for personal or economic gain using a blank check is the most sophisticated of all the concepts of the art of conversation and communication. The idea of cashing blank checks has been well documented from the time of early religious scholars of theology against people on personal levels to the current events pages of global news agencies in the twenty first century. As a general rule, the cashing of blank checks will always for the most part be a three way triangular relationship which will employ an act of betrayal by association. As a general rule the parties involved will consist of three distinct groups by name of association.

The first group: who will be the target of the accusation? The second group: accuser-betrayer who actually betrays private converted interest and shortly afterwards seeks or behaves in a manor that presents themselves as being a potential benefactor for personal, political, or financial gain even thou they were willingly participated in the continuation of the relationship. Finally the Payee: This person or group will in most cases always be a third party who is seeking some type of indirect receivership by the act of the betrayer. If the information is institutional, the information can be called private, privileged or insider information which can be seen as corruption and may be seen as acts of corruption. If the accusation is about an individual it may be interpreted and sold (in a media age) to the highest bidder on the street of public opinion as a "juicy story". A "juicy story" will always start out as an approved affair between all individual parties involved. In the initial stages of the relationships all parties concerned will be friendly, cordial, and agreeable as long as they could feel that they could get away with it; and their private self vested interest were not compromised or exposed to the public spotlight. However, the breakdown of the relationship begins to unravel when individuals in the group perceive the possibility of payment for privileged information and "bailing out" is a more beneficial and lucrative option than continuing the social engagement of the relationship. The act of betrayal by an accuser for personal or economic gain can be horrendous for he victim. The blank check cashers will attempt to piggyback off the targets name, position, perception of privilege, power, and influence or celebrity status.

On a personal level, the acts of blank check cashers can ruin individuals, their careers and destroy families. On a broader scale the cashing of blank checks can compromise company trade secrets and even include acts of espionage by employees to undermine the national security interest of a nation. Betrayal when enacted as a slick campaign will always be cloaked in disinformation from a serious liar against their focus target. The accusations can be so well planed that even seasoned professionals can be totally mislead about the reality of the issues, facts or events if the facts are not reviewed carefully. Betrayal cloaked in the idea of disinformation will always lend itself to the possibility of profiteering by the accuser at someone else expense for personal gain that is not justified.

Their may be truth to the charge or accusations of he check presenter but, the act of wanting economic reward for willingly engaging in bad behavior by all parties in association with the events leaves no doubt about the intent of the check presenters motives. Presenter's of blank checks always felt or knows that their window of opportunity as it relates to being able to continue a personal association with the target of discussion is rapidly closing. In addition, they also know that their ability to receive financial benefit form the personal association with the target is closing as well. The basic premise of the blank check concept is that the presenters of the check clocked themselves in legitimacy by close association to the target and as a result are able to confirm the events in question. The direct association by the presenters of the checks to the target establishes an authoritative position as it relates to their claim of legitimacy. If the check presenter approaches the target individual or group directly, indirectly with what many may call a "juicy story or secret information" and demands payment for silence in an attempt to gain financially, the act may be seen by law enforcement officials as blackmail or extortion which are both illegal.

Blank check presenters will always attempt to sell their stories to third parties who may have a vested interest in the topic and use their association as claim of legitimization by close association to the target or events in question. The process on the surface may be legal or illegal depending on how law enforcement views the events. But the spirit of the act will always be questionable if at the time of the events occurrence all parties involved freely participated in the act. If they had the chance or options to end their relationships but chose willingly to go along with their continued social engagement unabated legal lines of grey may have been crossed and extortion may have occurred.

On the business side of economic betrayal it may also manifest itself as hostile business takeover attempts by partners within the business. Or partners within the business that have outside vested interest who want to be part of the business. In both instances the offending parties in question always have some type of insider knowledge or close affiliation with the targeted individual or audience.

Level Four Lie: "Time Bandits"

The fourth level of lies deals with the concept of Time Bandits. Individuals who fall under this title are liars also if they make a habit of procrastinating with their work responsibilities on a consistent basis. The reason is that they will, as a rule, procrastinate on doing or completing their assigned task and in the end request others to help them fulfill production goals or personal needs.

In an effort to save their personal, family, or company interests, time bandits will have a tendency to wait until the last minute before asking for help, and as a result, they put everyone at risk. The reason why the Time Bandit is so dangerous is that they will steal the one commodity that no one can replace: their personal time. Each of us is given the same amount of hours in the day. No one has twenty-five or twenty-six hours in a day. Therefore, what you do with your allotted time is the most valuable commodity each of us has during our lifetime.

Master/Serious Types of Liars

These are living spiritual forces of darkness!

Head-walkers

Relationship Saboteurs

Rot-a-derpDestroyers

Be advised, once you have identified a person as being a master/serious liar, you must make every attempt to remove yourself from their presence. If you can see them with the naked eye or with glasses on, they are too close to you.

Types of Liars

Head-Walkers. I identified this group by this name because they (figuratively) walk on other peoples heads. The concept is that a head-walker will always put other people down in an attempt to promote themselves by stealing others' ideas. They will stifle to a certain extent individual expression, creativity, and independence at all levels from others. They do this because they fear that the expression of ideas by others may challenge their authority and they will lose control of any given situation. For the most part I have found that head-walkers will generally not become destroyers. They need the ideas of others around them to make themselves look and sound good in public or private places. Ultimately however, they fear that they will eventually be replaced by someone else who has a more moderate or democratic disposition when it comes to moving a concept or idea forward. Head-walkers are secretive by nature, but they may operate in groups depending upon the circumstances or issues at the moment. You will only be able to identify a head-walker by close association and observation over time.

Relationship Saboteurs: This group was identified as important because they will be individuals who are close to you. They can easily be friends, coworkers, or neighbors. They will tend to be people who know you well or work with you. However, they will be individuals who secretly spread rumors about your personal life, abilities, or intellect in an effort to undermine your good name.

Rot-a-derp Destroyers: Warning! Be advised, a true destroyer will have loyalty to no one but themselves or a select few. They will betray and sell out anyone, including their own parents, for a dime or a dollar if the price is high enough. Destroyers intentionally mislead others. Destroyers will always present their true colors in time by their words, actions, or both. The actions of a destroyer are always a total deception. In addition, there will be no rhyme or reason to their actions. They will have a tendency to both want and need to micromanage everything and everyone around them. This will include professional relationships, marriage relationships, business relationships, and personal relationships. This obsession with control will even extend to the point of telling the family dog when to poop.

As a result of this need to micromanage every aspect of any given project twenty-four-seven, they will eventually lose sight of the big picture from a corporate, organizational, or family perspective and drive all vested personal relationship interest into the ground.

In the Bible, these basic principles are fully explained under the concept of leadership styles. This chapter, 1 Samuel Chapter twelve, specifically addresses the acts that leaders will and will not do.

Individuals who, in my opinion from observation, demonstrate a number of these tendencies associated with individuals that initially start off as being relationship saboteurs and eventually become destroyers will fall into one of three of the following categories, if not both.

A. They are in management positions where they evaluate others.

B. They are in positions to green light projects, business, and organizational direction.

C. Depending on the circumstances of the time and place Rot-a-derp destroyers will as a general rule cloak themselves authoritatively over others by claiming any number of the following strategies in an effort to convince others of their self worth and logic of their beliefs and actions. The list is as follows: power by position or seniority, academic training, or political-social mandate of the people in an effort to convey legitimatization of their actions. When questioned by others on issues of ethical-moral behavior, legal conflict of interest or heavy handed (predatory) tactical methodical procedures; they will claim that it was done for the betterment of mankind. The reality however, in most cases will be that it will have all the markings of self vested interest of either a single individual or a powerful select few who will ultimately benefit from the overall effort of the or castrated lie and receivership of their desired want.

Destroyers act the way they do because they do not know their own God-given DNA blueprint formula for success. Your personal success is always interlinked with the actions of God and other people. You may be able to control 20% percent of your success directly; as it relates to your efforts of networking, volunteering etc.

But, for the most part, your efforts will be directly related to the favor of God and the help from other people who are in the right place at the right time. You will need this joint effort to assist you in the act of achieving personal success; whether it's personal, professional, or financial. Head-walkers, relationship saboteurs, and destroyers will know and understand this fundamental fact. To this end, it must be understood that destroyers are the most dangerous of all the types of liars. Destroyers can and often will be a combination of relationship saboteurs and head-walkers.

In addition to fulfilling all the acts of a serious liar, destroyers know what they are doing. Ignorance of their actions will not be an excuse. The actions of a destroyer will be intended to totally destroy those they dislike. Because of this internal feeling, the level of evilness a destroyer will demonstrate cannot be underestimated.

They will *not* demonstrate by words or action any consciousness in relation to either morals or ethics. When examining their behavior as it relates to their actions; destroyers, unlike the previously mentioned categories of relationship saboteurs and head-walkers, will generally operate on all five levels of a lie simultaneously: level one and two, avoidance, and time bandits.

As a general rule, destroyers will fulfill all the principles of a lie by their individual actions alone. Their actions always appear to be supportive, but are, in fact, a total deception. In the work or business environment, destroyers operate at their maximum levels when they realize that others around them are trying to meet deadlines in order to take advantage of opportunities that are time sensitive. They will be the people who let you down at the most critical point in time. Because opportunities in most cases for people are directly related to the fulfillment of task by hourly time and calendar dates.

Destroyers will intentionally delay or miss their mandate to deliver or finish task by the agreed date. They will have the skills, ability, time, and personal connections to complete the task and fail to come through with their assigned task. Destroyers can ultimately commit heinous crimes that human consciousness will find appalling. Destroyers are, or will be, as a general rule, people who are in your daily life. They may even be on your family tree. Although, destroyers can show up in your life by coincidence at the least opportune time, they are not one time associations.

Many will say that sometimes not getting what you want or getting your way will may prove be a good thing or blessing for you in the long run. This can be true; I am not arguing this fact. However, you will only know the reality of a situation when time runs its course. Personal reflection over time will always be 20/20 in relation to events in our lives, and God will always look out after you; unlike serious liars who are operating under the pretext of winning all the marbles. Destroyers do not have to obtain a receivership experience in order to gain satisfaction for their deeds. They will be pleased with the results of their action by simply negating an individual's or groups' forward progress in relation to them achieving success. They will be focused in the long run on breaking and destroying relationships among individuals or groups.

Destroyers always operate under the objectives of destroying relationships on spiritual, historical, and personal levels. Their actions-goals will be to destroy relationships to the point of being irreparable. Destroyers are the ultimate destructive forces outside of act of nature on planet earth.

Example: (Satan's influence on Adam and Eve in the Garden of Eden.)

Once you identify a destroyer; you will have to become very specific in your prayer life and ask God to remove the mountain (destroyer) in your way. If the damage has already been done, you will have to ask God to correct the injustice that has been committed against you. He will!

Anytime a destroyer acts to tear down another person or group and create "hard places" in peoples' lives, the pain they inflict on others will always be returned to them equal to the amount of pain they dished out against others if not more. This is another reason why you do not want to ever fulfill any of the first twenty principles of a lie.

The psychological metamorphoses of an individual from a head-walker into a relationship saboteur and ultimately destroyer will gradually manifest itself over a period of time. Exceptions to this rule will be that they feel this way instantly, the moment they meet someone who they perceive to be more successful than they are.

This is especially true if the destroyer is in a position of authority over others and they feel that they are more successful and have fewer responsibilities. The cost of involvement of dealing with relationship saboteur and destroyers will always prove too be extraordinarily high.

The cost of association will manifest itself in an individual's personal emotions, finances, and lost opportunity. Relationship saboteurs and destroyers intentionally mislead others. Destroyers will always present their true colors in time by their words, actions, or both. Destroyers act the way they do because they do not know their own God-given DNA blueprint formula for success. Your personal success is always interlinked with the actions of God and other people.

Earlier, I mentioned how I felt individuals became head-walkers and destroyers.

I came to this conclusion by observing individuals who I knew or students I taught. I noticed that people who appeared frustrated by others' success had a tendency to gravitate into behavioral patterns that they knew did not fall under the title of acceptable behavior according to society.

However, I realized that individuals who went down this road did this because they rationalized that means or methods, no matter what the cost, justified the end.

The obtainment of the desired prize made the effort logical if the end-state goal could be achieved and they believed that they could get away with it. If an individual feels that they can get away with something; they will automatically feel that they won't get caught.

Thus, individuals who reach the age of maturity (twenty-one years of age) can fall into a cycle of acceptance because they do not know there personal DNA model for success.

Your Personal DNA Formula for Success

Many readers at this point may be asking how you find your DNA success model.

For those of you who asked, I have good news: it's actually very simple; in fact, it's written in the palm of your hand and maybe on the bottom of your feet if you're an athlete. However, there will also be an intellectual aspect to your skills/gifts that are not necessarily academically-based as well.

The first task will be to ask your parents (if you're lucky enough that they are still alive), or older brother and sisters, or close family relatives who knew you when you were young; "Mom/Dad, what were the things I really did well as a kid between the ages of two and eight years of age?" Your parents will know (generally speaking) because they raised you. They may tell you that you have a gift for art, music, reading, writing, putting things together, winning friends, playing sports, etc. The reason why this age is important is because educational research has proven that children between the ages of two and eight will demonstrate very high levels of creativity. Once kids get past the fourth or fifth grade, they become engaged in what educators call a truly structured curriculum and creativity dramatically drops off.

The establishment of curriculum codes/subjects was designed to give students exposure to a number of subjects so that they could be functioning literate adults. Many times, the curriculum, although broad in scope, teaches to the weaknesses of students and not their strengths. Entrepreneurs and motivational speakers all agree that people should be in fields and work in areas that are their strengths. When you are working from the strengths of your natural gifts and talents, you will most likely be successful in your field of interest. It is important to remember that these gifts will not be academically based. They are naturally yours, and you don't need necessarily a license to practice them. But be advised that in some professions, you do need a license to practice your hobby/gifts if it becomes your profession.

Examples would be cosmetology, medicine, law, teaching in a public school, certified auto mechanic; the list can go on and on. Check with your state licensing bureau for more information.

The second way I have found that people can discover their DNA success model is to look in their family tree. There is a good chance that somewhere on your family tree you will find people who had interests similar to yours.

You may discover that you had or have a great uncle who is a doctor, race car driver, or designer, and you have a similar interest. You may have to go back several generations to find people who worked in fields that you are interested in.

The third way to discover your DNA success model is to examine the things that you like to do. Once this is done, you can go to a community college or employment agency and they may have tests you can take that can help you find your interest skills and abilities. The importance of doing this is that once you discover your true skills, you'll start working to develop your interest.

Once you develop your interest; you'll find that you will not need to lie on other people, become a headwalker, relationship saboteurs, or even destroyers. Soon after you discover what you believe to be your true calling. Don't be surprised to find that your personal plate of success will be overflowing with rewards just from the good deeds and works you have done for others.

Characteristics of Destroyers

Individuals who are true destroyers will, as a general rule, display several overt characteristics, which an individual should be aware exist. An interesting point to notice is that many of these characteristics are revealed early in an individual's life. The first one is that destroyers will have a tendency to have a controlling personality. They will want and need to micromanage or control everything and every one around them. Their self-image is or appears to be me, myself, and I.

Destroyers will create divisions within the ranks of people in groups or organizations in an effort to divide and conquer by misleading others in an effort to achieve their own personal goals. In addition, people who you will come to know as destroyers will always be individuals who you cannot please, satisfy, or agree with on any issues.

Because the actions of head-walkers, relationship saboteurs, or destroyers are selfish; their actions will always be unpredictable. They will not do anything that will benefit their neighborhood, community, city, state, nation, or humanity on a global basis.

Individuals who advance the quality of life for humanity on a national or global basis often win *Nobel Peace* prizes; destroyers will not win this prize because they will not be willing to devote serious time to any cause or even lay down their life for the cause, as it relates to the betterment of mankind. Destroyers can be the proverbial wolf in sheep's clothing. They need not always appear to be menacing from their outward appearance.

But their actions, words, and policy decisions will always speak for themselves.

The title of destroyer can manifest itself on many different levels.

On The School Yard

In our public and private schools, administrators and teachers have always known the effects a bully can have on other students. In our early grades, where kids are enrolled in grades K-12; destroyers are known as school bullies. Administrators and law enforcement take the actions of bullies to be very serious. They do not and will not underestimate these individuals or their actions. The actions of bullies can provoke timid individuals to carry out aggressive acts against innocent people as a method of revenge for their personal pain.

The Area of Romance

In romantic or marital relationships, the actions of destroyers can be classified under the title of spousal abuse. Spousal abuse can take the form of psychological as well as physical battery.

Professional Relationships

In the adult professional, business, or working environments destroyers; will focus their efforts on character assassination and economic depravity against the individual or the audience in question. They may attempt to define themselves as task masters in an effort to gain acceptability by others.

Adult Relationships

It must clearly be understood that task masters and destroyers can never be under any circumstances one and the same. They are diametrically opposed to one another. (Opposite) Task Masters will build people up; bring out the best in others; be supportive; and officer constructive criticism to help others in a non-offensive manner.

Destroyers

Destroyers only tear people down. Criticism from a destroyer will always highlight only shortfalls in others, groups, or cultures. Their word will never be kind. They will never see or admit to the successful accomplishments of anyone or any group. History has proven that the actions of a destroyer on any level at any age can lead to physical murder.

Task Masters

In fairness, I must state that not all controlling personalities are destructive. Some, in fact, can be good, if they push to bring out the best in others. An example of this type of personality would be a task master. Task masters will be supportive of individual expression (dependent on the task/job), and not tear down the people around them.

They will not have the "me, myself, and I" focus as their internal motivation for the group.

Task masters will provide structure for the overall good of the group in an effort to achieve success for everybody in the group to the best of their abilities. Examples of this concept can be found in the teaching and the military profession. To this end as a counter balance, I identified another group of people who I categorize as *mentors* or *stepping stones*.

Mentors and
Stepping Stones

These individuals not only lift themselves up by doing good deeds; they also lift everyone else around them up by being supportive and giving advice for free or even leading (if they are able). When individuals seek them out for advice or to help them because they are confronted with challenges that are perplexing, and they are not able to solve the problems themselves; a person who is a mentor or stepping stone will help.

These individuals will *not* have private agendas that negatively affect others. The importance of seeking out and surrounding yourself with people who are mentors or stepping stones is imperative to an individuals overall achievement of success.

These kinds of people can be found in churches, civic organizations in your individual communities, professional associations, and family members. Support from these individuals, church affiliations, and civic organizations will help keep your mind sharp and open to new ideas and corrective constructive criticism if need be before you begin the process of creating serious lies about other people. With this in mind, I have revised my definition of a lie so that individuals can see for themselves that they will not want to become participants in acts of lying in an effort to achieve success.

"New Definition of a Serious Lie"

A serious lie is a pre-planned act or strategy whose author has a clearly defined end-stated goal from its conception. The use of knowledge, falsehood, and deception are used to take advantage of the ignorance of its intended victim or group. The goal of obtaining ownership of the valued object of interest will be the primary focus of the author actions; whether the operational process is overt (public) or covert (secretive) in nature. A serious lie will involve a theft of some type at some level. In addition, an attempt to not only break, but also destroy coveted relationships between parties of interest will be enacted in an effort to ensure the gaining of a position of power. The theft need not be one-dimensional. It can be a combination of many objectives, which include monetary, time, ideas, intellectual property, physical property, trust from others, loss of freedom, peace of mind, even life itself. Because the theft can manifest itself on many levels, it will always transcend many levels of personal interaction between the members of the selected parties of interest. This group will include personal, business, individual opportunities, social standing among members of the community or professional organizations, and religious, romantic, and family encounters. Serious liars will always enact the act of betrayal. Because these people are, as a rule, close to each other (intended target) in their work, play, social, romantic, educational, or professional environment; they will bring legitimacy to their actuations in an attempt to convince others of their concerns and beliefs.

Residual Effect of a Serious Lie

A. Serious lies are called serious because the effects of the lie from the author have severe impact on the individual or the audience identified as the intended target of the lie.

B. Resolution of issues associated with a serious lie will not, as a given rule, be a quick fix in relation to clearing up the matters of dispute.

C. The serious lie by it's vary nature is designed to create long range, if not permanent setbacks for the individual or audience who the focus of the allegation is originally intended for.

The Fall from Grace of a Liar Will Be a Call to Justice

The fall from grace of a serious liar will be a rapid and the landing will be hard. Depending upon the issues, the fall from grace will also be a private and possibly public humiliation depending on people and issues involved. When the trumpet of justice sounds, the clap of thunder from God may be silent or take many forms, but God will always place the exclamation point of disapproval behind the actions of serious liars and destroyers who are the true authors of the Madness. His judgment will be a definitive answer and it will be a very public statement.

The Six Stages of a Lie

In the following diagram, I have laid out what I have to come to know and believe as the fundamental progressive steps of a lie. For the reader who takes the time to read, understand, and master the steps of a lie; it may help many individuals to identify the stages the lie will be in and plan an effective attack or defense to lessen the damaging affects of the authors of a lie.

The Six Progressive Steps of a Lie

Stage # 1 _____
Individual
Author/initiator
Of the Lie
(Level #1–3)
(Covert by nature)

Stage # 2 _____
Small group conversations
Method of dissemination
Newspapers, internet, pod cast
Television, Radio etc.
These are the physical forms
A lie must take to gain
legitimacy and support.
(Level # 2–3) (Overt by nature)

Stage #3
allegation
large group
Public Speculations
(Level # 2–5)
(Overt by nature)

Stage # 4 _____
Legal inquiry
Grand jury investigation
(Level 4–6)

Stage # 5 _____
Trail/Legal Process
(Level # 1–5)
(Overt by nature)

Stage #6
Vindication or acquittal
(Level #1–6)
(Overt by nature)

The Twenty-One
Principles of a Lie

(Master/Serious Lies by Nature)

Quote 1 for Principle 1
"A man whose word will not inform you at all what he means or will do is not a man you can bar gin with. You must get out of that man's way, or put him out of yours!"

> Thomas Carlyle (1795–1881). "The Hero as King," On Heroes, Hero-Worship, and the Heroic in History, 1841.

Quote 2 for Principle 1
"I always make it a point of business ethics never to tell a lie unless I think I can get away with it."

> Kenneth Cook and Kerry Cook.
> "Makers," 4,1983

Quote 3 for Principle 1
   "Everybody is ignorant, only on different subjects."
                        Will Rogers Reader'sDigest

Principle 1 (first aspect): The initiators of a lie must always work from the assumption or premise that the intended victim, group, or audience (public), as a rule, is unaware about the behind-the-scenes aspects of the accusation, and is operating in a spirit of ignorance. The hope of the author of a serious lie is that the target does not know the facts, their civil rights, legal rights, the issues, or the reality of the situation in relation to the relevance of time and impact of their decisions on their further situations.

What gives the master skilled authors of a serious lie their legitimacy is the ignorance of the targets or audience.

This belief *must* be in place (Levels 1–4) before the initiator of a serious lie can reasonably expect to convince others and gain supporters to move the allegations past the oral discussion stage in an attempt to gain both legitimacy and longevity of the issue.

The (second aspect) of a lie under principle one is that being educated makes an individual immune to the tickets of a master skilled liar. A master skilled liar is good at what they do because they have been telling lies for a long time. As a result, they will know what words to use, how to sit in a chair, stand, make or give facial expressions, and a host of external attributes to sell themselves and convince others of their sincerity and the utility of their agenda, needs, or position on any topic of interest that they specialize in.

The only defense against a skilled master liar is that the intended victim knows the facts, their rights, or the issues before this type of liar approaches them. An individual must be educated about the facts of an issue at hand before they meet a master skilled liar to avoid becoming a victim.

> "There are three kinds of lies: Lies, damned lies, and statistics."
>
> > Benjamin Disraeli (1804–1881). Attributed by Mark Twain, April 1904, Mark Twain's Autobiography, 1.246, ed. Albert Bigelow Paine,1924

> "All men can be led to believe the lie they want to believe."
>
> > Italo Bomolini
> > *Words of the Wise by Rosemarie,* Sky Publishing, New York, New York

Principle 2: The lie is the methodology used to insure and guarantee the desired outcome of a course of action that will have a negative effect on its intended victim, group, or selected audience (Stage 1, page 156).

This tactic is most employed by employers and political propaganda in war or political related campaigns. Employers who use this strategy do so in an attempt to find a way to get rid of workers who they wish to terminate. In an attempt to find some way to guarantee that they will be able to remove or get rid of selected employees they feel are in too strong of a legal position of seniority, knowledge, or relationship to powers of leadership to openly challenge them outright; they will create situations where the employee will find it difficult to work and cite them for poor performance in relation to doing their job duties. The problem with this approach is that any good lawyer who knows the law of management or human resources will be able to point to facts in the body of case law and established research finding to tear down this argument.

Governments will use this tactic to employ psychological terror in the minds of the enemy and the people in the surrounding area in an effect to remove their fighting spirit. This act in military terms is called dissemination of misinformation. The authors of a serious lie will always create the madness-environment for the legitimatization of the lie.

> "Unless a man feels he has a good enough memory, he should never venture to lie."
>
> Montaigne, Essays 1580
> *Internet Dictionary of Quotations 3rd edition*

Principle 3: Innocent as well as serious lies do not happen by chance. They all have an author and they always have an ultimate objective (Stage 1, page 156).

The author of any lie that is classified as a serious lie always has a stated goal. This objective makes the telling of the lie in a certain way mandatory in the liar's attempt to achieve the lie's goals as legitimate.

"Show me a liar, and I'll show thee a thief."
John Clarke (1596–1658)

Principle 4: A serious lie always involves a theft of ownership using deception as a referred method of recourse.

In addition to the aspect of a theft, the element of cost or opportunity may occur as well as either a byproduct or direct residual effect of the attempt to obtain ownership.

In addition, if the actions of a serious liar do not result in obtaining the desired goal to the benefit of the liar; the third aspect of the lie will be on the part of the initiators of the lie to try to break and destroy the coveted relationship between the parties of interest to the liar's advantage. In both theory and fact, this is a defacto theft in its most basic principle, because the author of the lie will either directly or indirectly gain an advantage position for their efforts. Defacto: Actual or functioning whether legal or not. (Stage 1, page 156)

"No one ever lies. People often do what they have to do to make their story sound right."
William H. Ginsburg. In Francis X. Cline's "Day of Facing the Nation, Meeting the Press, Etc." *New York Times*, 2 February 1998

Principle 5: Initiator of a lie will always try to disguise the lie as a popular belief or the guiding principle by wish a lie obtains either longevity, legitimacy, or both. (Stage 3, page 156)

Historically, people who are most subjective to this principle have a tendency to be public personalities whether they are politicians, musical or movie celebrities, political activists, or anyone who authorizes and special interests feel threaten the established order or position of the ruling group. This strategy need not be associated with national personalities alone; it can occur within the neighborhood of common citizens who deal with each other or work in the same office.

Many times the attackers will attempt to disguise themselves by adopting the cover of civic organizations, professional associations, newspaper editorials, television commentaries-documentaries, talk radio, or a host of other communication channels.

"The ultimate measure of a man is not where he stands in moments of comfort and convenience, but where he stands at times of challenge and controversy."
Martin Luther King, Jr. *Harper Book of Quotations*

Principle 6: The lie is designed to create a stumbling block in a person's life.

(Stage 3, page 156)

In order for a lie to be successful, the author of a serious lie must create situations where the target or audience has to slow down and has to adopt a reactionary posture to the situations, events, or allegations. This act will give the author of a serious lie time to solidify their resources to support their effort. The problem is that there will always be someone or a group of people who know that the facts that they are trying to sell or convince the public of are not true and they will be called on to defend their actions.

> "Gossip is when you hear something you like about someone you don't."
> Earl Wilson, *The Harper Book of Quotations*

> "No gossip ever dies away entirely, if many people voice it: it too is a kind of divinity."
> Hesiod *The Harper Book of Quotations*

Principle 7: A lie is designed to tear a person down (Stage 2, page 156).

In addition to creating stumbling blocks in a person's life, the author of a serious lie will have to create an environment where others will agree with them that the targeted individual or group deserves the treatment they are receiving and thus the lie is true. This action will always manifest itself as an allegation attempting to prove the author's claim to be right. When addressing this issue, it is interesting to note that four basic principles of the Bible as stated in Exodus chapter twenty. (The Ten Commandments)

Once someone starts fulfilling the principles of a Serious Lie they automatically break four of God's Ten Commandments:

A. Thou shalt not bear false witness against thy neighbor.

B. Thou shalt not covet thy neighbor's house, thou shalt not covet they neighbor's wife, or his man-servant, or his maidservant, or his ox, or his ass, or any thing that is thy neighbor's.

C. Thou shalt not commit adultery. In a marriage, relationship and adulterer will be operating on almost all of the levels of the twenty-one principles of a lie.

D. Thou shalt not kill. When someone know-ingly tells a falsehood about someone else they are using and operating from a position using education and knowledge about the facts of any given situation to inflict psychological harm to another person. This makes the act intentional and mean-spirited by nature and automatically breaks all three of the aforementioned Biblical principles listed above.

This act of murder, unlike its physical form, becomes a living spiritual murder, because the individual or group has to react or live with the consequences of the lie.

"Whenever there is a crowd there is untruth."
Soren Kierkegaard, *Harper Book of Quotations*

Principle 8: A lie is designed to increase a person's burdens (Stage 3, page 156).

As the allegations become more focused, the intended victim will realize that it will become more difficult to operate and trust those around them in matters of confidentiality.

"Moral indignation is jealousy with a halo."
H.G. Wells *Reader's Digest*

"I never came across anyone in whom the moral sense was dominant who was not heartless, cruel, vindictive, log-stupid, and entirely lacking in the smallest sense of humanity. Moral people, as they are termed, are simple beasts."
Oscar Wilde *Reader's Digest*

Principle 9: A lie is created to question the moral or intellectual abilities of its intended victim in the eyes of others.

The end purpose will be to raise allegations about issues that it's intended victim, or group, will have to defend against (Stage 4–6, page 156).

Principle 9 is applied in times of political elections and appointment confirmations, whether they are in government or private business. In addition, this type of lie can also happen in the office environment at work and the community relationships within neighborhoods. Liars who operate in this arena are very dangerous. They will generally stop at nothing to achieve their goal. The depth of lawlessness will, as a rule, have no limits, and there is no conscious effort to use a sense of justice or boundaries of decency in carrying out their actions.

"Words, once they're printed, have a life of their own."

Carol Burnett *Reader's Digest*

"The medium is the message."

Marshall Mc Luhan
Harper's Book of Quotations

"Americans detest all lies except lies spoken in public or printed lies."

Edgar Watson Howe, Ventures in Common Sense (1919), 2.6 *International Thesaurus*

"Writing is one of the easiest things: erasing is one of the hardest."

Rabbi Israel Salanter *Harper Book of Quotations*

Principle 10: All lies have oral and physical aspects associated with the momentum of the falsehood 30% oral/ 70% physical. A lie will always manifest itself in a physical form once it goes beyond the rumor stage (Stage 2, page 156).

In order to gain and obtain legitimacy, a lie at some point will have to appear in one or several of the following communication mediums. Written: Computer generated e-mails, handwritten letters-notes, newspapers articles, television documentaries, video, radio, or any physical means of communication. The psychology of creating a written account of a lie in the eyes of the master skilled liar is to gain legitimacy from its readers. Individuals, groups, or organizations that print or disseminate these statements if proven untrue are thus legally responsible for acts of character assassination on the grounds of slander (Stage 2–3, page 156).

> "Beware of false prophets, which come to you in sheep's clothing, but inwardly they are ravening wolves."
>
> Ibid 7:15

> "Whenever there is a crowd, there is untruth."
> Soren Kierkegaard *Harper Book of Quotes*

Principle 11: The author—perpetrators of a lie will always have allies, whether they are willing, unwilling, or unknowing accomplices (Stage 2–3, page 156).

Once the author of a lie disseminates the lie to the public, it will take on its own momentum. Individuals, whether they know it or not, will become either willing or unwilling accomplishers in the promotion of the lie. Only informed, knowledgeable individuals will be able to discern facts and fiction in the propaganda attempt to create doubt in the minds of less informed individuals or groups about the truth of the issues.

> "Nothing gives such a blow to friendship as the detecting another in an untruth. It strikes at the root of our confidence ever after."
>
> William Hazlett (1778–1830). *Characteristics in the Manner of Rochefoucault's Maxims*, 199, 1823

Principle 12: All lies have some order of betrayal (personal) by close parties involved, who are associated with them in exchange for perceived legitimacy of value of the accusations (Stage 3–6, page 156).

Because the author of a lie must be able to prove legitimately an effort to ensure both acceptance and longevity of a false accusation; the person who initiates the lie will most likely be a close confidant to the intended target or group of the accusation.

In almost every account of stories that appear in newspapers, magazines, or audio/video accounts of an act of wrongdoing; the accuser will position themselves in such a way as to be creditable in relation to the accounts of the facts as they relate to the issue.

"The more lies are told, the more important it becomes for the liars to justify themselves by deep moral commitments to high-sounding objectives that mask the pursuit of money and power."
Bertram Gross (1912–1997), *Friendly Fascism: The New Face of Power in America,* 9, 1980

Principle 13: The authors or perpetuators of a serious lie never see either the moral or the ethical conflict of their acts. They will always defend their actions by claiming it was done and justified for the good of the group, institutions, society, or even the nation. (Stage 4–6, page 156).

The old adage of the right hand never knowing what the left hand is doing in relation to a serious lie will never hold up in the long run. Individuals or groups who participate knowingly in a serious lie always know what they are doing. Individuals who participate in this activity, at the serious lie level will always have a secret agenda. This self-motivation effort will block the major players who have the most to either gain from perpetuating the lie to morally or ethically acknowledge the wrong of their actions.

They will always cite reasons for their actions as being for the good of some third party as a way to deflect attention away from themselves as the true beneficiaries of the lie effort. When confronted with public inquiry, the authors of a serious lie will present a single individual or selected group as the front men/women, or special interest as the public face of the campaign. Behind the scenes, there will always be a group of operatives who will be creating and directing the offensive charge to both sell and legalize the lie to the public. The problem will come, however, at some point when either an individual or selected group members will have a conscious conflict and reveal the true nature of the operation as well as its operators and intended goals.

> "I loathe like Hell's Gates the man who thinks one thing and does another."
> Homer (eighth century b.c.) *The Iliad,* 9,310, tr.
> E.V. Rieu, 1950

> "One man lies in his words, and gets a bad reputation; another in his manners, and enjoys a good one."
> Thoreau, *Journal,* June 25, 1851

Principle 14: The actions of a liar are easy to spot; Their actions never match their words. Their words never match their actions (Stage 5–6, page 156).

"You cannot make a person do something that is not in their heart, the feeling in a person's heart will always, within time, give them away."

"Liars can't make anyone orally respond to suggestions that they know are not true." Although the threat of cohesion can be used to encourage someone to take a public or private position that is not to his or her liking;

the spirit of justice will always reveal itself within a short time as to the true aspects of a lie and its author. A classic example of this would be an experience I had while attending a jazz performance at a local events venue. On this day, a young couple walked up to where I was standing and took an empty table next to me. After a short time, the man went to the bar area and returned with a silver bucket of ice and a bottle of wine. Within a few moments, he once again left to get something from the food section area. While he was gone, the woman who he was with asked me if I wanted to have a bottle of wine. I thanked her, but refused the offer and informed her that I did not drink. I thought the offer was unusual, considering she was in the company of another man. I asked her if that was her husband; she replied that it was. At that moment, I realized that the relationship between these two was not a relationship of husband and wife.

In fact, the man was trying to impress the woman and it appeared that they were on a date. Husbands will not make a mistake like this at anytime in public with issues involving their wives. People who are married or have been dating for any period will know what the other person likes or dislikes. The principle of fourteen: Their actions never matched their words, and their words never matched their actions that were played out to the letter in plain view. The question at this point becomes what was the end-state goal that this woman was trying to accomplish.

"His words were softer than oil, yet they were drawn swords."

Psalms 55:21 *Harper Book of Quotations*

Principle 15: The author of a lie must always have some sort of personal association with its intended target in order to claim public legitimacy or their acquisition (Step 1–6, page 156).

In all cases, personal connection to the target or audience is essential for a liar to sell his or her version of a lie. The personal involvement created a legitimacy of being on the scene or acting as an eyewitness. The problem is that the author of this type of serious lie will always trip themselves up in the regurgitation of the lie to others. Times and dates never match and additional information will always be absent from the original concept story.

"The prophets prophesy lies in my name: I sent them not ... they prophesy unto you a false vision and ... the deceit of their own hearts."

Bible, Jeremiah 14:14

Principle 16: Because a lie is a deception, designed to gain the attainment of an object of desire by the author of a serious lie; they will attempt to use one or all three of the following methods to obtain ownership.

A. Trickery: To get the owner to willingly give up their ownership position.

B. Persuasion: Do this or else (blackmail).

C. Cohesion: Use physical force to achieve the end goal (Stage 1–6, page 156).

"Repletion does not transform a lie into a truth."
Franklin D. Roosevelt, Radio Address,
October 26, 1939

Principle 17: A level two lie must always become public in order for it to gain momentum and accrue some sort of legitimacy (Stage 2–6, page 156).

Because level two lies must carry with it public support, the author of this lie will invariably try to have it accepted by mainstream distribution channels. When this happens, the distribution channels are subject to and accountable for the damage of any false allegations they publish if the issue or story proves to be false. A classic example would be the Richard Jewell story. Richard Jewell was the man accused of killing several people in the Olympic Park bombing in Atlanta during the 1996 Olympics.

Shortly after he was identified as being a hero, allegations started about whether or not he was in fact a person of spurious interest. In a split moment, his life went from being a hero to being a criminal, and he spent years trying to clear his name. It must be remembered that in time Richard Jewell was acquitted of all charges brought against him and the smearing of his name. He eventually got a job in law enforcement before his death and served with great distinction.

> "Woe to those who call evil good and good evil."
> Isaiah (eighth century b.c.) Isaiah 5:20

Principle 18: The liar or liars (if possible) will never show his or her true colors until the deed, deal, or act has been performed to the point of satisfactory finality; if they can get away with it (Stage 1–6 page 156).

Because the goal of a serious lie must appear, to be in the public interest, the authors of a serious lie must, and will at all costs, attempt to hide their true interest in the issues at hand. The revealing of the individuals who may become the benefactors of the lie's success will not want to reveal themselves because of legal charges that may arise and possible imprisonment if their true interests were revealed. The problem with this is that insiders who know the truth about the issues will always catch them and have a stake in protecting their position of interest or control no matter what the outcome of the organized effort.

> "A single lie destroys a whole reputation for integrity."
> Baltasar Gracian (1601–1658). The Art of
> Worldly Wisdom, 181, 1647,
> Joseph Jacobs, 1943

Principle 19: Lies in most cases always involve intellectual, ethical, or moral questions.

The lie will never question a person's athletic ability to perform a given task if they are honest. Athletic ability can be proven by observation and longevity to play a sport.

In light of medical advances in science, the initiation of random drug testing of both humans as well as animals such as racehorses has been instituted to maintain the legitimacy and integrity of sports in recent years. This act or process legitimizes the premise that lies are restrained to the intellectual or moral doctrines of society.

"A lie has speed, but truth has endurance."
Edgar J. Mohn *Reader's Digest Quotations*

Principle 20: All lies run their course in time. The result will always be total failure and exposure of its goal if it's not true.

Common sense or law will in most cases always prove false allegations untrue and require the allegations in most cases to be dismissed if they cannot be substantiated by fact. Exceptions to this rule will be if the emotions of people one way or another have charged the topic at hand in the media.

The result of this action will or may prevent the acceptance of reason or logic in the minds of the audience to accept the facts of the attempt to sell the lie.

"The punishment of the liar is that he eventually believes his lies."

Elbert Hubbard (1856–1915). The Note Book of Elbert Hubbard p.47, comp. Elbert Hubbard II, 1927

Principle 21: The liar will always have to subconsciously live with their acts of betrayal and falsification. All liars will be, in time, exposed for who they are, their motivation, and injustice they cause others in either the court of public opinion or a court of law on earth. However, it is guaranteed that one day all liars will stand before the All Mighty in heaven, who most people know as God and have to answer or account for their actions on earth.

Strategies to Fight a Serious Lie

"We lie to ourselves, in order that we may still have the excuse of ignorance, the alibi of stupidity and incomprehension, poses which we can continue with a good conscience to commit and irate the most monstrous crimes."

Aldous Huxley (1894–1963). "Words and Behavior," The Olive and Other Essays, 1936

To fight the good fight against a serious liar, there are several methodologies one should and must consider when attempting to find solutions against the clever tactics of a liar to illegally gain control of an object of interest or destroy converted relationship.

The first is to seek religious advice in how to defeat the spirit of hidden agendas.

Secondly, seek counsel from close trusted friends or family members if you are able.

Finally, be prepared to fight in the courts of law if guided and need be.

Personal Reflection

Since the beginning of time and recorded history, whether it is oral or written, the concept of success has been both an admired and elusive quality for most people who have lived on this planet. Everyone wants to be successful. In fact, it is a gift that every one has on the inside of them and even written on the palms of their hands and feet. The big problem is that most people are not successful because they have not tapped into or are not using the gifts they have been given. Not everyone can be an Olympic athletic, movie star, singer/musician, writer, businessperson, medical doctor, dentist, artist, engineer, educator, police officer, firefighter, etc.

In my sixteen years as a classroom teacher, I have concluded that every person on earth has at least two natural gifts that are not academically related to personal success.

If you are able to get degrees, or certification in your area of expertise or natural abilities, and you enjoy what you do, you are very lucky. Most people do not realize that success in all cases will not only carry with it blessings to the individual, nation, group, or family members; but also the recognition, attention, and envy of others who may not be supportive of your good fortune. If you are successful or good at any task, someone will notice. If you are the best minimum-wage hourly worker, someone will notice your abilities.

The attention will naturally follow not only individuals, but also churches, family business, institutions, corporations, and nonprofit organizations. You do not have to become a millionaire or president of the United States, recipient of the *Nobel Peace Prize,* or get public recognition in the local or city newspaper, to receive unwanted negative attention. The negative attention can come from the most unlikely sources that most people do not even think of when they have to deal with the reality of defending themselves against the allegations of liar. The host of characters is not in any way exclusive. It can range from members of your own neighborhood community, coworkers on the job, or even family members who feel in some way that you are unrealistically indebted to them because of blood relationships. To this effect, everyone is subject to the possibilities of being the targeted interest of a liar.

Because success will always carry with it some since of personal accomplishment, it will always get the attention of others. People who are successful, no matter what their endeavor, always have an aura about them that other people can notice. It does not have to take the form of pride; but there will be a sense of peace of mind and confidence about them that others will notice. If you go to the check-out counter of any grocery store or supermarket stand and look at the news rack of magazines, you will undoubtedly notice that all the magazines only have successful people on them or people who society feels are making a difference in the lives of others.

You will almost never see a homeless person on the cover of a magazine unless the magazine is addressing an issue of homelessness or that particular person has committed some type of crime, or is the focus of negative publicity to deflect attention from the true culprit, which in fact can be governmental policy, employment policies, loan criteria, or any array of topics that helped create the current conditions that the homeless live in today. Everyone has value, the homeless are not an exception. Although their current living condition may be because of bad choices they personally made, there are always two sides to every story.

If someone was to talk to these people; the average person may be surprised to find out that many of these individuals in fact are in their current predicament because of the actions of others who had secret agendas that where not to their benefit. The many forms that success may take may be the joy of doing things for others, achieving a personal life-long goal; monetary or a host of other measures that the individual may use to measure there personal growth in comparison to others that they personally interact with, read about, or admire. Psychologists have discovered that of all the qualities man has, the need for self-actualization is the strongest instinct a person will have after the basic needs for food, shelter, and water have been met. If a person cannot reach or obtain their desired goals in life, they may resort to underhanded tactics to achieve there desired in goals.

The mythological process most will follow will be creating deception or falsehoods in the eyes of others about the target victim who they secretly admire and want to be like (sand in their shoes).

Because the motivation of the author of a lie is a major, determining point of reference in whether or not the actions of individual or groups can be viewed as innocent or serious, the following principal understanding must be remembered.

Concluding Principles
for Thought

"All lies involve two fundamental concepts. The first is that all lies involve some aspect of a cover-up (concealment of the truth)."

The second concept acknowledges that people who tell serious lies operate from the same psychological perspective as bank robbers, thieves, extortionists, conmen/women, etc.

They all feel that they can get away with it. The deciding factor every person must make when dealing with someone who is a liar is to be able to determine if in fact the lie that was told to them is an innocent lie or a serious lie and what is at stake.

Because a serious liar feels that they can get away with the act they are trying to perpetrate; *they will automatically believe that they will not get caught.*

The purpose of my writing of this book came because of being the, target personally, of well orchestrated campaigns by former employers, business partners, friends, and people who were in a position that I thought were respectful or supportive. I assumed that they would act in a sense of fairness. In fact, in the end, they proved to be not only disloyal, self-gratifying, unethical, and unprofessional; they proved to be committers of living spiritual murder and many were actually law breakers. In short, my walk though the gutless of adversity has allowed me to claim legitimacy and to confidently address the tactical methodical of serious liars. The need to read and understand the psychology of serious liars is vital in any attempt to create defensive strategies needed to protect your blessings from an experience point of view.

To this end, I wrote this book to be a stepping stone in an effort to help others accomplish several major objectives when confronted with acts of a liar. Recognize that a lie (depending on its purpose and who the author is) will be in most cases an act of wickedness designed to have a negative impact on its selected target or audience. The first, defensive strategy to remember is to stay mindful in prayer once you become aware of those around you who are acting in a manner of self-promotion or to obtain some type of benefit at the expense of others by using a lie to accomplish what they cannot do on their own without the help of others in an attempt to claim legitimately. Be specific in your prayers as to what you want God to do to relieve you of the attacks:

A. Recognize what a lie is, its levels, strategy, and end-state goals.

B. Identify the possible theft/breakage attempt of the actions of a master/skilled liar.

C. Remember that the battleground of all lies is in the mind.

D. Set up your own business for additional streams of income that will allow you to survive if the challenges of a lie become overwhelming from a financial standpoint. This will allow you to save and protect your blessings, should you ever have to travel through a long valley in time, in the process of clearing your name.

E. Recognize that your actions, as well as the actions of a liar, will be judged in the end.

This judgment may or may not come by your peers on earth, but is guaranteed to come when they stand before God.

Be assured that any individuals who knowingly participate with a group in the creation, execution, and receivership of valued interest as a result of using knowledge to enact a serious lie will all fall rapidly (as a group) from grace.

Reference

1. Holy Bible The Old Testament King James Version Revelation Seminar 1976 Keene, Texas
2. International Dictionary of Quotations Third Edition Margaret Miner & Huynh Rawson A Signet Book 2000
3. Readers Digest Quotable Quotes Wit and Wisdom for All Occasions 1997
4. Concise Oxford American Dictionary: Oxford University Press New York, New York 2006
5. Merriam Webster's Desk Dictionary 1995
6. Webster's II New College Dictionary 2005 Houghton Mifflin Company Boston, Massachusetts
7. Random House Webster's Dictionary 4th 2001 Random house Publishing Group 1745 Broadway, New York, N.Y. 10019

8. Webster's New World Dictionary and Thesaurus Second Edition 2002. Wiley Publishing, Inc, Cleveland, Ohio.

|LIVE

listen|imagine|view|experience

AUDIO BOOK DOWNLOAD INCLUDED WITH THIS BOOK!

In your hands you hold a complete digital entertainment package. In addition to the paper version, you receive a free download of the audio version of this book. Simply use the code listed below when visiting our website. Once downloaded to your computer, you can listen to the book through your computer's speakers, burn it to an audio CD or save the file to your portable music device (such as Apple's popular iPod) and listen on the go!

How to get your free audio book digital download:

1. Visit www.tatepublishing.com and click on the e|LIVE logo on the home page.
2. Enter the following coupon code:
   7ea2-6f29-a5e6-8cdd-3d15-b7a1-b7ff-3d4c
3. Download the audio book from your e|LIVE digital locker and begin enjoying your new digital entertainment package today!